GOD'S WORD

GOD'S WORD

READING THE GOSPELS WITH GEORGE MARTIN

Our Sunday Visitor Publishing Division
Our Sunday Visitor, Inc.
Huntington, Indiana 46750

ISBN: 0-87973-954-1
LCCCN: 98-65864

Cover design by Monica Watts
Printed in the United States of America
954

For Jim Manney

Contents

Abbreviations for Books of the Bible

Old Testament

Genesis	Gn	Proverbs	Prv
Exodus	Ex	Ecclesiastes	Eccl
Leviticus	Lv	Songs of Songs	Sg
Numbers	Nm	Wisdom	Wis
Deuteronomy	Dt	Sirach	Sir
Joshua	Jos	Isaiah	Is
Judges	Jgs	Jeremiah	Jer
Ruth	Ru	Lamentations	Lam
1 Samuel	1 Sm	Baruch	Bar
2 Samuel	2 Sm	Ezekiel	Ez
1 Kings	1 Kgs	Daniel	Dn
2 Kings	2 Kgs	Hosea	Hos
1 Chronicles	1 Chr	Joel	Jl
2 Chronicles	2 Chr	Amos	Am
Ezra	Ezr	Obadiah	Ob
Nehemiah	Neh	Jonah	Jon
Tobit	Tb	Micah	Mi
Judith	Jdt	Nahum	Na
Esther	Est	Habakkuk	Hb
1 Maccabees	1 Mc	Zephaniah	Zep
2 Maccabees	2 Mc	Haggai	Hg
Job	Jb	Zechariah	Zec
Psalms	Ps	Malachi	Mal

New Testament

Matthew	Mt	1 Timothy	1 Tm
Mark	Mk	2 Timothy	2 Tm
Luke	Lk	Titus	Ti
John	Jn	Philemon	Phlm
Acts of the Apostles	Acts	Hebrews	Heb
Romans	Rom	James	Jas
1 Corinthians	1 Cor	1 Peter	1 Pt
2 Corinthians	2 Cor	2 Peter	2 Pt
Galatians	Gal	1 John	1 Jn
Ephesians	Eph	2 John	2 Jn
Philippians	Phil	3 John	3 Jn
Colossians	Col	Jude	Jude
1 Thessalonians	1 Thes	Revelation	Rv
2 Thessalonians	2 Thes		

Preface

I fell in love with God's word in Scripture in 1964. It began with a Lenten resolution to read Scripture for fifteen minutes each day. I had never read the Bible; I had to go out and buy a copy to read. As I read day by day that Lent I discovered a new world, the world of Scripture. More importantly, I began to experience God's word in Scripture as his word to me. What I read had implications for my life; my Scripture reading provided a springboard to prayer and became part of my relationship with God. When that Lent was over, I kept on reading.

I started writing about Scripture almost by accident later in that decade. I was responsible for arranging facilities and sending out a notice for a monthly gathering. If the notice didn't fill the page, I added a brief reflection on Scripture at the end, a paragraph relating something that had struck me in my reading. The single paragraph grew to two paragraphs and three paragraphs, until eventually I was mailing out a page-long meditation on Scripture with a meeting notice tacked on as a P.S.

When *New Covenant* magazine began in 1971, the editor invited me to submit my meeting-notice Scripture reflections as a monthly column. The meeting has long been discontinued, but the column has endured, passing the three-hundredth installment mark in 1997. The purpose of the feature remains the same as when I began writing thirty years ago: to provide some insight into the meaning of a passage of Scripture, with an eye to its relevance for our lives as followers of Christ.

Sometimes I write about a passage from the Old Testament, sometimes from the New: It depends on what insights I may have had into Scripture the previous month. Sometimes as the writing deadline approaches I find myself praying, "Lord, give me some insight into your word in Scripture — and soon!" Looking back, I find that I have written more about the four Gospels than the other books of the Bible, which is as it should be: the Gospels are the preeminent witness to the life and teaching of Jesus Christ, and the bedrock documents of our faith. They are my favorite books of the Bible.

The Gospel meditations gathered together in this book focus on Jesus and our lives in him. While they are loosely grouped by theme they do not pretend to be a systematic exposition of the Gospels. Some meditations overlap others, for they were written as individual reflections without much thought to what I might have written a decade or two earlier. I present them simply as meditations on what the Gospels tell us about who Jesus is, and what he did and taught, and on some of the implications for those who would be his followers.

These reflections originally appeared in *New Covenant* magazine, save for "What Did Jesus Look Like?" which appeared in *Catholic Digest*.

George Martin

1

What Jesus Is Like

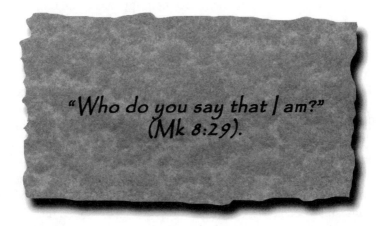

"Who do you say that I am?"
(Mk 8:29).

Born in Bethlehem

Jesus was born in Bethlehem of Judea,
in the days of King Herod (Mt 2:1).

Astronomers tell us that the sun is one of one hundred or more billion stars in the Milky Way galaxy, and the Milky Way is in turn one of about one hundred billion galaxies in the universe. Some galaxies are so far away that their light has taken billions of years to reach us, even though light travels at the speed of one hundred eighty-six thousand miles per second.

It is virtually impossible for us to comprehend a universe of such magnitude and age. We gauge distance and time in terms of our own experience. Traveling sixty-five miles an hour on a freeway we can understand — but one hundred eighty-six thousand miles per second? The distance from St. Louis to Chicago is within our grasp, but not the distance light travels in a year, much less a billion years.

We worship a God who created this unimaginably vast universe. If current theories are right, God created it as an infinitesimal speck of near-infinite energy that exploded into all we see today. What is God like, that he could summon forth the vastness of space and time from a spark? If we can't comprehend the universe, how can we even begin to comprehend its Creator?

God had mercy on us and revealed himself to us in terms we can understand. If our minds cannot comprehend the infinite, then God would assume finitude, to give us a glimpse of who he is.

God did so in Jesus, who "was born in Bethlehem of Judea, in the days of King Herod" (Mt 2:1). We know where Bethlehem is: not in some other galaxy light-years away, but just south of Jerusalem, thirty-five miles inland from the eastern shore of the Mediterranean. We know when King Herod ruled: not billions of years in the past, but only two thousand years ago. In Jesus, God entered into our space and time.

Measured against the vastness and age of the universe, the birth of Jesus took place here and now. What are the few thousand miles that might separate us from Bethlehem compared to the distance to even the nearest galaxy? What are two thousand years compared to the billions of years since creation? In cosmic terms, the Creator of the universe comes to us in Jesus right here, right now.

Yet the mystery of God remains even in God-become-human. He who is born in Bethlehem in the days of Herod is the one through whom the universe was created (see Jn 1:3; Col 1:16; Heb 1:2), come to live as a creature in his own creation. Is it easier for us to grasp a Creator whose handiwork is itself beyond our comprehension — or to grasp that this Creator took on our humanity and lived among us? Is it easier to imagine God dwelling beyond the stars, or lying in a makeshift cradle in Bethlehem?

For those who embrace the mystery of the Word become flesh, Jesus is a window onto God. Paul calls him "the image of the invisible God" (Col 1:15). The Letter to the Hebrews speaks of him as the radiance of God's glory, bearing the very imprint of God's being (see Heb 1:3). Jesus expressed it simply: "Whoever has seen me has seen the Father" (Jn 14:9). Whoever looks on Jesus sees the one through whom the galaxies were created; whoever listens to the voice of Jesus hears the voice of their Creator (see Jn 14:10). Jesus is Emmanuel — "God is with us" (Mt 1:23).

The Magi had a star to guide them to the place of Jesus' birth (see Mt 2:9); we have a whole universe of stars to bear witness to the meaning of his birth. At Christmas we celebrate the awesome mystery of the infinite God, the Creator of all that is, entering into our here and now, taking on our flesh and blood, speaking to us in human language, bridging the gap between us and himself.

What Did Jesus Look Like?

"Is he not the carpenter?" (Mk 6:3).

The Gospels do not describe what Jesus looked like. They proclaim him to be the Son of God and Savior of the world, and that he is, regardless of whether he was tall or short, long-haired or bald. Artists have portrayed him in different ways through the centuries — most often as looking like the people of their own culture.

We can surmise, though, that Jesus looked like the people of his culture: He was to all appearances a first-century Middle-Eastern Jew. Some of his neighbors in Nazareth found him so ordinary in appearance — so much like them, in other words — that they could not accept that he was anything more than a first-century Jew.

How did first-century Middle-Eastern Jews look? They were on the average shorter than people are today. Some of their features have probably been handed down to some of the Middle-Eastern Jews of today. But since body build and facial features differ even within ethnic groups, this doesn't tell us much about Jesus as an individual.

The Gospels do, however, give us some important clues about the general physical appearance of Jesus. The first clue is that Jesus was a carpenter (see Mk 6:3) and the son of a carpenter (see Mt 13:55). Immediately images of carpenters come to our minds — perhaps shirtless young men framing a house on a hot summer day. But is this the kind of carpenter Jesus was?

The Gospels use the Greek word *tekton* to describe the occupation of Jesus and Joseph, a word Bibles translate as *carpenter*. But a *tekton* was one who worked with any hard and lasting material, including stone as well as wood. Houses in Nazareth usually had stone or mud-brick walls; wood was used sparingly for roof beams, doors, and door frames. Did Jesus work with stone as well as wood? He probably did. One estimate puts the population of Nazareth at the time of Jesus at one hundred twenty to one hundred fifty people. How many woodworkers and stone masons did such a village need? Perhaps Joseph & Son served most all the construction and handyman needs of Nazareth, from building a wall to repairing a chair.

There were, obviously, no power tools at the time of Jesus. Wooden planks and stone blocks had to be cut and shaped with hand tools. Since trades were passed from father to son, Jesus would have grown up helping Joseph hew beams and wrestle foundation stones into place — everything that a village *tekton* was called upon to do. Recently I visited an archaeological dig in Israel, excavating first-century Bethsaida. A group of young, muscular workmen were moving a stone from the wall of a house, and it took all their strength. As a *tekton*, Jesus may have strained with similar stones.

I therefore think that Jesus was a rather rugged man, with heavily callused hands and well-developed muscles. I don't know whether he was stocky or lanky, but he was strong. He could put in a full day of hard manual work, day after day.

When I was in college, I applied for a shovel job on a pipe-line crew. The foreman looked at my uncallused hands and shook his head; it was obvious that I was not used to such work. After some pleas, I got the job anyway, and a good many blisters that summer. Had it been Jesus at my age applying for the job, the foreman would have taken one look at his work-hardened hands and hired him on the spot. I doubt Jesus would have developed any blisters.

I don't mean to imply that Jesus was a common laborer: A *tekton* was a skilled occupation, requiring the mastery of a variety of tools and materials. Jesus could have crafted a better table or chest than I could ever hope to, even with power tools.

Another clue to the general physical appearance of Jesus is found in what some call "the fifth Gospel," the Holy Land itself. When we look at a map of the Holy Land, it has the appearance of being flat. But as every pilgrim discovers, the Holy Land is very hilly. It is a steep climb up eighteen-hundred-foot-high Mount Tabor, the traditional site of Jesus' transfiguration. It is a long upward journey from Capernaum to Caesarea Philippi in the foothills of Mount Hermon, the site of Peter's confession of faith. There is no level path from Galilee to Jerusalem; there are few level streets in Jerusalem itself.

Yet Jesus walked these routes, and walked them repeatedly. For the ordinary person in the ancient world, travel meant travel on foot. Travelers would average fifteen to twenty miles a day, depending on the terrain. To go from Galilee to Jerusalem for pilgrimage feasts, which devout Jews did three times a year, would have meant four to seven days of such walking, each way. John's Gospel tells us that Jesus went to Jerusalem for major feasts.

Hence our image of Jesus must be of a man who could walk seventy to eighty miles over the course of a few days to worship and teach in Jerusalem, and then walk the same distance home — so that he could continue his ministry by walking from village to village in the hills of Galilee. Jesus said that he had nowhere to lay his head (see Mt 8:20): How many nights in the course of his travels did he sleep in a field, wrapped in his cloak? Jesus repeatedly went up mountains to pray — a natural way of getting some privacy for someone used to hiking steep terrain.

Jesus was in very good physical shape by modern American standards. He earned his living by the strength of his arms and back; he carried out his ministry on the strength of his legs. We should bear this in mind as we read the Gospels.

When Jesus speaks of a house built on rock withstanding wind and floods better than a house built on sand (see Mt 7:24-27), he speaks as one who had laid his share of foundations. When he speaks of a stone rejected by builders being made a cornerstone (see Mk 12:10), he echoes his own experience in sorting building blocks and choosing cornerstones.

Jesus said, "I am meek [or gentle] and humble of heart" (Mt 11:29). But we should not use this verse to form a mental image of Jesus as a soft, delicate person, someone who might have made his living by posing for holy cards. Rather, Jesus may have needed to reassure his listeners of his gentleness because he looked like a sturdy village *tekton.*

But gentle he was. Parents brought their infants to Jesus "that he might touch them" with his callused hands (Lk 18:15). Jesus wept at the death of his friend Lazarus, wept so profoundly that bystanders exclaimed, "See how he loved him" (Jn 11:35-36).

Jesus' physical ruggedness should be kept in mind as we read the accounts of his passion and death. Matthew and Mark tell us that Pilate, the Roman governor, had Jesus scourged (see Mt 27:26; Mk 15:15). Roman scourges were generally leather thongs with pieces of bone or metal at their ends to tear through flesh and muscle. The Gospels do not tell us how severely Jesus was scourged, but they do tell us that soldiers later forced Simon of Cyrene to carry Jesus' cross.

What was normally carried was not the entire cross, but the crossbeam; the upright portion of a cross was a post permanently implanted at a place of execution. The crossbeam would be laid across the shoulders of a condemned man for him to carry to the place of crucifixion. But according to Matthew, Mark, and Luke, Jesus needed help carrying the crossbeam, and Simon was made to carry it instead of him. As a carpenter, Jesus had undoubtedly carried many beams in his life, some for sizable distances, and some of them far heavier loads than this crossbeam. But he was now incapable of bearing its load; that is an index of how horribly his muscles had been torn by scourging.

God could have chosen to send his Son to be the adopted son of someone with a desk job — a scribe, or perhaps even a tax collector — so that Jesus would assume that occupation. But in God's plan, Jesus was a *tekton* with a body hardened by work, and it was that body he gave up for us on the cross.

A Day in the Life of Jesus

The apostles gathered together with Jesus and reported all they had done and taught. He said to them, "Come away by yourselves to a deserted place and rest a while." People were coming and going in great numbers, and they had no opportunity even to eat. So they went off in the boat by themselves to a deserted place. People saw them leaving and many came to know about it. They hastened there on foot from all the towns and arrived at the place before them. When he disembarked and saw the vast crowd, his heart was moved with pity for them (Mk 6:30-34).

Once Jesus emerged from his forty days in the wilderness, he was rarely alone again. There was usually an unending stream of people coming to him: blind beggars and bent women, leprous outcasts and argumentative lawyers, the demon-possessed and mentally impaired, the curious and the hostile, sinners and self-righteous, the diseased and the disturbed.

Jesus was incessantly besieged by people in need, whether on the road (see Mk 10:46-52) or in the home of a friend. "When Jesus returned to Capernaum after some days, it became known that he was at home. Many gathered together so that there was no longer room for them, not even around the door" (Mk 2:1-2). "He came home. Again [the] crowd gathered, making it impossible for them even to eat" (Mk 3:20).

Jesus could not even enjoy a quiet evening by himself after a hard day's work. "When it was evening, after sunset, they brought to him all who were ill or possessed by demons. The whole town was gathered at the door. He cured many who were sick with various diseases, and he drove out many demons" (Mk 1:32-34). Nor was he left in peace in the early morning hours. "Rising very early before dawn, he left and went off to a deserted place, where he prayed. Simon and those who were with him pursued him and on finding him said, 'Everyone is looking for you' " (Mk 1:35-37).

It is never recorded that Jesus turned anyone away. No matter how tired he might have been, no matter who came to him, no matter how unreasonable their demands, Jesus responded with compassion. When he looked at those who came to him, "his heart was moved with pity" (Mk 6:34).

Jesus expected his disciples to do the same. Jesus commissioned his followers to perform the same works he performed (see Mk 6:7-13), and he asked them to love as he had loved (see Jn 13:34-35; 15:12-17).

Jesus imposed no particular acts of penance on his followers: He did not ask them to fast, as did other spiritual leaders (see Mk 2:18). But inevitably the hardships of Jesus' life overflowed onto his disciples. The greatest hardship must have been the incessant crowds of those clamoring for help. If there was any particular penance in being a follower of Jesus, it was the penance of constant availability and lack of privacy. If there was any particular distinction to being known as a follower of Jesus, it was the distinction of being expected to do what he did.

When Jesus, Peter, James, and John came down from the Mount of Transfiguration and rejoined the rest of the disciples, "they saw a large crowd around them and scribes arguing with them" (Mk 9:14). Why was the crowd gathered around the disciples? Seeking healing from them as they sought healing from Jesus: "Teacher, I have brought to you my son possessed by a mute spirit. . . . I asked your disciples to drive it out" (Mk 9:17-18).

It is not easy to be expected to do the same things as Jesus. It is not easy to become known as someone who helps others, for to the extent we are really helpful, many more may come to us in need. It is not easy to have our time taken over by those who are hurting or hungry or thirsting for a message of hope.

Neither was it easy for Jesus. But he didn't complain: He was about his Father's work, as he invites us to be (see Jn 5:17; 20:21).

Jesus' Powerlessness

[He] came to his native place . . . [and] began to teach . . . and many who heard him were astonished. They said, "Where did this man get all this? . . . What mighty deeds are wrought by his hands! Is he not the carpenter, the son of Mary, and the brother of James and Joses and Judas and Simon? And are not his sisters here with us?" And they took offense at him. . . . So he was not able to perform any mighty deed there, apart from curing a few sick people by laying his hands on them. He was amazed at their lack of faith (Mk 6:1-6, shortened).

Why was Jesus unable to perform mighty deeds in his hometown of Nazareth? The obvious answer is because of the lack of faith he encountered: "And he did not work many mighty deeds there because of their lack of faith" (Mt 13:58). But this answer demands exploration.

Did the disbelief of the townspeople of Nazareth rob Jesus of his supernatural powers? Would he have been unable to turn water into wine in Nazareth, as he had done in Cana? This cannot be. Jesus' power came from his being the Son of God; it was not a magical quality that switched off and on at the city limits. If we look only at Jesus' abilities, whatever he was capable of doing anywhere he was capable of doing in Nazareth. And in fact he did cure some sick people in Nazareth by laying his hands on them (see Mk 6:5).

What then was the problem in Nazareth? I believe the key lies in the kind of "mighty deeds" that Jesus performed. Nowhere do the Gospels describe Jesus performing a miracle except to meet some human need. He heals the sick, he frees the possessed, he saves his disciples from storms, he feeds hungry crowds, he provides commercial fishermen with a good catch, he even provides a coin for a necessary tax payment (see Mt 17:27).

Yet despite his ability to perform mighty deeds, Jesus does not indulge in gratuitous displays of his power. He does not float down from the pinnacle of the temple (see Mt 4:5-7), he does not hurl mountains around like tennis balls (despite Mt 17:20), he does not paint stripes on the moon. Jesus surely could have performed all sorts of spectaculars that would have awed the crowds, but he did not work wonders except to meet human needs.

We should also note that Jesus made no invariable demands on those he helped. He welcomed the faith of those who believed he had the ability to heal them, but he also healed those who demonstrated no faith, simply out of compassion for them — even those who did not ask to be healed (see Lk 13:10-16), even those who did not know who he was (see Jn 5:1-13).

What then happened in Nazareth? Jesus met with not only lack of faith but with positive disbelief. People took offense at who he claimed to be. The people of Nazareth were sure they knew who Jesus was, because he had grown up in their midst and had done carpentry work for them. Most of them rejected the possibility that he was anything other than a carpenter. The only kind of needs that they were willing to bring to Jesus might have been broken chairs and sagging doors.

The result was that Jesus did few mighty deeds in Nazareth, since he performed mighty deeds in response to human needs. He was quite capable of doing in Nazareth what he did elsewhere, but the people of Nazareth generally refused to bring their needs to him. Jesus found this refusal amazing. Even if he didn't demand faith as a condition for healing, he at least wanted more than positive rejection.

If this understanding of the incident at Nazareth is correct, then the only thing that prevents Jesus from helping us is our rejection of him, our refusal to come to him with our needs. Disbelief makes Jesus powerless only in the sense that he can't do for us what we won't let him do. We should turn to Jesus with as much faith as we can muster, but never hold back from him because we feel we do not have enough faith. Jesus simply wants the opportunity to help us.

Jesus and Scripture

When the feast was already half over, Jesus went up into the temple area and began to teach. The Jews were amazed and said, "How does he know scripture without having studied?" (Jn 7:14-15).

Scholars were a specialized profession in ancient times. They were men who knew how to read and write: Hence, one title for them was "scribe." They had studied under an older scholar as their master, and in turn taught others: Another title scholars therefore bore was "teacher."

Being a scholar was normally a full-time profession requiring long preparation. The book of Sirach describes various ordinary occupations, such as farmer, blacksmith, and potter, and then contrasts the scribe to them. Only those with the leisure to study could become scholars:

> Whoever is free from toil can become a wise man.
> How can he become learned who guides the plow . . .
> whose every concern is for cattle?
>
> How different the man who devotes himself
> to the study of the law of the Most High! (Sir 38:24-25; 39:1).

This specialization of occupations helps us understand the amazement of the people of Nazareth when Jesus began his public ministry. "He began to teach in the synagogue, and many who heard him were astonished. They said, 'Where did this man get all this? What kind of wisdom has been given him? . . . Is he not the carpenter?' " (Mk 6:2-3). The people of Nazareth were surprised that this Jesus who had been doing their carpentry work should suddenly begin acting like a teacher.

Jesus' background was a source of surprise in Jerusalem as well. When he began to teach in the temple precincts, the Jews wondered, "How does he know scripture without having studied?" — that is, without having studied under someone (see Jn 7:15). They were amazed that Jesus knew the Scriptures without having been trained by a rabbi; they were amazed that Jesus claimed to understand the Scriptures even though he was not a scholar.

We are probably less surprised by Jesus' knowledge of Scripture. After all, we might think, Jesus was God: He knew everything. But this overlooks his full humanity. Because he fully shared our human condition, Jesus had to learn by the same slow painful process we learn (see Lk 2:40, 52). He had to read through the books of the Old Testament, scroll by scroll, in order to grasp their meaning. Jesus did not have an infused knowledge of Scripture, but learned the meaning of Scripture through reading and reflection and prayer. As fully divine, Jesus was completely receptive to the graces of the Spirit that enlightened his reading. But Jesus' knowledge of Scripture began with his own careful reading of the inspired texts.

Jesus was thoroughly immersed in the words and meaning of Scripture, and it was in light of Scripture that he understood his own mission. His first sermon in Nazareth was a proclamation that he fulfilled a prophecy of Isaiah (see Lk 4:14-21). He told his followers that he would be put to death in fulfillment of the Scriptures (see Lk 18:31-33). He criticized those who rejected him because they failed to understand the Scriptures and what they said about him (see Jn 5:39-40, 45-47). And after his resurrection, he opened the eyes of his followers to understand what he had been trying to teach them all along: that he was the fulfillment of Scripture (see Lk 24:25-27, 44-48).

Jesus was not a Scripture scholar by profession, but someone who read and pondered the word of God, and understood his own life in light of that word. In this, Jesus is an example for us, who likewise are not professional scholars but bricklayers and housewives, nurses and salesmen. There is certainly a place and important role for scholars: Sirach's words in praise of them are, after all, a part of inspired Scripture. But everyone who follows Christ, scholar or not, is addressed by the word of God. Each of us should treasure the Scriptures no less than Jesus; each of us should study them as Jesus studied them; each of us should understand the meaning of our lives in light of Scripture, as did Jesus.

Merciful Loving-kindness

While Jesus was having dinner at Matthew's house, many tax collectors and "sinners" came and ate with him and his disciples. When the Pharisees saw this, they asked his disciples, "Why does your teacher eat with tax collectors and 'sinners'?" (Mt 9:10-13 NIV).

On hearing this, Jesus said, "It is not the healthy who need a doctor, but the sick. But go and learn what this means: 'I desire mercy, not sacrifice.' " (Mt 9:10-13 NIV).

It should be no surprise to us that Jesus used Scripture in his preaching and teaching, the same Scriptures that we read as the Old Testament. Thus Matthew's Gospel presents Jesus twice quoting Hosea 6:6 in order to make a point: once to defend his practice of associating with sinners (see Mt 9:13) and once to criticize the Pharisees' quickness to condemn (see Mt 12:7). Since Jesus twice quotes God's words, "For I desire mercy, not sacrifice" (Hos 6:6 NIV), it would behoove us to "go and learn the meaning" (Mt 9:13 NIV) of these words.

We can first note that Matthew's Gospel was written in Greek, and that Matthew therefore has Jesus quoting a Greek translation of the words of Hosea. In this translation it is "mercy" that God desires, using the same Greek word for mercy that Jesus will use in the beatitude, "Blessed are the merciful, for they will be shown mercy" (Mt 5:7 NIV). Jesus shows mercy to sinners (see Mt 9:10-13), a mercy that the Pharisees fail to extend (see Mt 12:1-7).

If we look up Hosea 6:6 in our Bibles, however, we will find that most translations speak not of mercy but of love as God's desire: "It is love that I desire, not sacrifice." The Hebrew word that Hosea used to express what it was that God desired carries a broad range of meaning: It can be translated as love, kindness, mercy, grace, goodness, favor, and benevolence. When the book of Hosea was translated into Greek, the Greek word for mercy was chosen to express what Hosea had said in Hebrew. But Hosea's Hebrew word carried a far broader meaning than mercy, and we should keep this broader range of meanings in mind.

Hosea's first listeners would have immediately grasped what it was that God was asking for: He was asking them to have the same loving-kindness toward him that he had toward them. On Mount Sinai God had proclaimed that he was "a merciful and gracious God, slow to anger and rich in kindness and fidelity" (Ex 34:6), and it was precisely this loving-kindness that God was in turn demanding from his people through his prophet Hosea. One scholarly translation of Hosea 6:6 even renders it, "I desire loyalty, not sacrifice," making it clear that the love that God asks for is first of all our love for him.

However, our love of God in return for his love must overflow into love for all those he loves. God asks us to behave as he behaves toward us. As we receive his kindness, mercy, and love, so we must be kind, merciful, and loving to others.

This was what Jesus was inviting the Pharisees to reflect on in the two encounters in Matthew's Gospel in which he quoted the words of Hosea to them. The Pharisees took great pains to carry out what they understood to be the obligations God had imposed on them. But they overlooked something very basic: God's merciful loving-kindness toward us, and his call to us to have the same merciful loving-kindness toward each other.

When Jesus welcomed sinners to himself and ate with them, he was carrying out his Father's work, for his Father was a God of great mercy and loving-kindness. When the Pharisees criticized Jesus for associating with sinners, or when they harshly judged the disciples for foraging grain on the Sabbath, they showed that they understood neither the merciful kindness of

God, nor how they were to reflect this merciful kindness in their own attitudes and actions.

And what of us? Have we learned the meaning of the words "What I desire is merciful loving-kindness and not sacrifice?" Or in our attempt to render God his due, do we look down on those whom we judge to fall short of his standards? Have we pondered on God's love for us as the standard of what our love should be? Have we meditated on the example of Jesus as our model of the meaning of love?

Jesus' Compassion

As he went ashore, he saw a great crowd; and he had compassion for them, because they were like sheep without a shepherd; and he began to teach them many things (Mk 6:34 NRSV).

In those days when there was again a great crowd without anything to eat, he called his disciples and said to them, "I have compassion for the crowd, because they have been with me now for three days and have nothing to eat" (Mk 8:1-2 NRSV).

The Gospel of Mark twice describes Jesus feeding a crowd of hungry people (see Mk 6:30-44; 8:1-9). The first incident takes place when Jesus tries to get away with his apostles for a needed rest, but people nevertheless find them (see Mk 6:31-34). Rather than be upset by the crowd's intrusion, Jesus has compassion on their spiritual needs and teaches them, afterwards feeding them as well. In the second incident, Jesus is moved with compassion by the hunger of those who have been following him for three days, and he feeds them.

Several things stand out in these two incidents. One is that Jesus' instinctive reaction is compassion. He is not irritated that a crowd of people intrude on his quiet time; rather, he is moved with compassion for them. He does not say to the crowds, "You should have had the foresight to pack a lunch"; he has compassion on their hunger.

Another lesson: Jesus is concerned about all our needs, physical as well as spiritual. He was moved with compassion by the empty stomachs of those who came to him as well as by their spiritual emptiness, and he fed them in both body and spirit.

In doing so, Jesus was more than simply a kindly fellow wandering around the hills of Galilee. He is the image of the unseen God (see Col 1:15); to gaze on him is to see his Father (see Jn 14:9). Jesus' attitude toward us is therefore God's attitude toward us. In Jesus' compassion, we are given a privileged glimpse of God's compassion.

That makes it worthwhile to reflect on the compassion Jesus had for the crowds. The Greek word Mark used to describe Jesus' compassion is vivid: *splangchnizomai*, a verb meaning "to have pity," comes from the noun *splangchna*, meaning internal organs. The King James Version rendered this word as "bowels of compassion" (1 Jn 3:17). We might prefer to say "heartfelt mercy" or "moved with compassion from the depths of one's being." Jesus did not have just a twinge of pity for those who came to him in need; he was profoundly moved with compassion for them, moved from his innermost being.

Jesus' spontaneous heartfelt compassion is an index of God's compassion for us. God is not mildly interested in our well-being; God is passionately concerned for us. He sent his Son to give us a glimpse of just how compassionate he is for us.

The word "compassion" itself gives us another clue to God's attitude toward us: *Compassion* comes from the Latin for *suffer with*. God demonstrated his compassion for us by sending his Son to be one of us and to take our suffering upon himself. In Jesus, God suffers with us.

Suffering is a mystery. Why does a good God allow there to be so much suffering on this earth — particularly the suffering of innocent people caught up in wars and ravaged by famines, stricken by diseases, and subject to untimely death? There is no glib answer to this question. There is, however, the image of Jesus on the cross. God has not abolished our suffering, but he has entered into it. God's compassion for us finds its ultimate and most vivid expression in his suffering with us in his Son.

Closeness to God

He took Peter, John, and James and went up the mountain to pray. While he was praying his face changed in appearance and his clothing became dazzling white (Lk 9:28-29).

Then they came to a place named Gethsemane, and he said to his disciples, "Sit here while I pray." He took with him Peter, James, and John, and began to be troubled and distressed (Mk 14:32-33).

It would be difficult to juxtapose two scenes from the life of Jesus that are in more apparent contrast than his transfiguration and his agony in the garden.

Jesus' transfiguration is the preeminent biblical example of a "mountaintop" experience: His appearance becomes radiant in prayer (see Lk 9:29), and he hears God commend him as his beloved Son (see Mk 9:7). Peter is so filled with joy that he suggests putting up tents so that they can stay there longer.

Jesus' agony in the garden is seemingly quite opposite. Jesus is troubled and distressed, "sorrowful even to death" (Mk 14:34). "He was in such agony and he prayed so fervently that his sweat became like drops of blood falling on the ground" (Lk 22:44). Peter makes no suggestion that tents be erected to prolong this scene.

We must wonder how Jesus could have such completely different experiences in prayer. Surely, we might think, anyone who has had an experience like the transfiguration should be forever immune to the kind of agonized prayer Jesus experienced in Gethsemane. It is hard for us to even keep these two scenes in our minds at once.

Yet there is good evidence that that is precisely what we are intended to do. There are too many parallels between the transfiguration and the agony in the garden for their similarities to have been accidental. They demand being understood together.

The setting of both is a mountain (see Lk 9:28; 22:39). In both incidents, Jesus goes there to pray (see Lk 9:28; Mk 14:32). The Father of Jesus figures importantly in both scenes: as the One who acknowledges Jesus as his beloved Son during the transfiguration (see Mk 9:7), and as the One whom Jesus calls out to as his "Abba, Father" during his agony (see Mk 14:36).

Both events speak a powerful word to us about what it meant for Jesus to be the Son of God, fully human and fully divine. Both therefore also speak to us about what it means to imitate Christ and be joined to him. The transfiguration was an anticipation of the glory of the risen Christ, a glory we hope to share when we join him in resurrection. In his agony in the garden he embraced the way of his Father which led to resurrection, a way we must also embrace.

Both moments give us a privileged glimpse of Jesus' intimate relationship with his Father. We might think that Jesus was much closer to his Father on the mountain of transfiguration than during his agony in the garden. But that is to take too psychological a view of these two events.

If I understand the clues that the Gospels give us, I believe it is preferable to believe that Jesus was even closer to his Father in his agony than in his exaltation. It is easy to embrace God in a moment of glory; it is much more difficult in a time of anguish. In which moment was he more totally submissive to his Father's will? In which moment did his Father most long to reach out his arms and embrace him?

Perhaps geography itself provides a hint regarding these two events — not a proof, certainly, but the kind of hint that the Fathers of the Church delighted in exploring. The traditional site of Jesus' transfiguration is Mount Tabor in Galilee; the traditional location of Gethsemane is an olive grove near the foot of the Mount of Olives, in the Kidron Valley. Mount Tabor rises 1,850 feet above sea level. But because Jerusalem lies in the hill country, the Garden of Gethsemane, even though it is in the Kidron Valley, is about 2,200 feet above sea level. Paradoxically, the valley of the agony is nearer the heavens than the peak of transfiguration. And we can note that the place of Calvary is higher than either of them.

Are we also nearer to God during our moments of anguished prayer than we are during our mountaintop experiences? Are we closer to him when we cry out in pain, "Abba, thy will be done," than when we are flooded with grace and all is easy? The answer rises above Calvary, and it is a cross.

Show Us the Father

Philip said to him, "Master, show us the Father, and that will be enough for us." Jesus said to him, "Have I been with you so long a time and you still do not know me, Philip? Whoever has seen me has seen the Father. How can you say, 'Show us the Father'?" (Jn 14:8-9).

We can sympathize with Philip wanting to see God. Our own faith would be strengthened immeasurably if we were granted a glimpse of God, if just once the heavens opened and we were able to see him in whom "we live and move and have our being" (Acts 17:28).

But physical eyes by their nature can only see physical things. And since God is pure spirit, "no one has ever seen God" (Jn 1:18). He who is spirit must take on matter and enter into our physical world in order to be visible to our physical eyes. And that is what God did in Jesus:

"The Word became flesh
and made his dwelling among us,
and we saw his glory,
the glory as of the Father's only Son" (Jn 1:14).

Still, what did Jesus mean when he said, "Whoever has seen me has seen the Father" (Jn 14:9)? For it is clear that many saw Jesus without realizing that they were seeing God. Many saw Jesus heal the sick and heard him preach, and yet walked away from him (see Jn 6:66). Even some of Jesus' relatives had no faith in him (see Jn 7:5). Many who looked at Jesus saw only a carpenter from Nazareth.

There is seeing, and there is perceiving. Some can look at a painting and see only colors on a canvas; others can perceive a masterpiece. Some can look at Jesus of Nazareth and see only a carpenter; others can perceive who he really is. In the vocabulary of John's Gospel, seeing, believing, and knowing are related: True sight comes from faith; to know Jesus is to perceive him through eyes of faith.

Who is Jesus, that to see him is to see the Father? Jesus is the Word become flesh, the Son of God sent from the Father to reveal the Father (see Jn 1:18). To see Jesus, to perceive who he really is, is to see someone who was sent by the Father. Correspondingly, the Father is revealed as the one who sent Jesus among us, and sent him out of love:

"For God so loved the world that he gave his only Son, so that everyone who believes in him might not perish but might have eternal life. For God did not send his Son into the world to condemn the world, but that the world might be saved through him" (Jn 3:16-17).

God "gave his only Son" in two senses: gave him to us as the Word made flesh, and gave him up to death on a cross for our salvation. To perceive who Jesus is, is to perceive his Father's love in sending him and giving him up for our sakes.

We do not know Jesus unless we know him as the one sent by God. We do not see God in Jesus unless we perceive Jesus as a demonstration of God's love for us. To look at Jesus of Nazareth and see his Father means to perceive Jesus as the Word made flesh, sent into the world for our sake, and it means to perceive as well why he was sent: because God loves us, and wants us to have eternal life.

In speaking of the Word made flesh, the author of John's Gospel claims that "we saw his glory" (Jn 1:14). When did Jesus reveal his glory "as of the Father's only Son" (Jn 1:14)? It was above all on the cross, for Jesus calls his death as his hour of glorification (see Jn 12:23). To see Jesus on the cross is to see his Father's love for us; to perceive what happened on Calvary is to be given that glimpse of the invisible God we desire.

2

The Gospel of Grace

"I give them eternal life, and they shall never perish. No one can take them out of my hand" (Jn 10:28).

Good News

The beginning of the gospel of Jesus Christ [the Son of God] (Mk 1:1).

After John had been arrested, Jesus came to Galilee proclaiming the gospel of God: "This is the time of fulfillment. The kingdom of God is at hand. Repent, and believe in the gospel" (Mk 1:14-15).

The English word *gospel* comes from Anglo-Saxon *godspell*, which means *good news*. This is a literal translation of the Greek word *evangelion* used by Mark to describe his book and to tell us that Jesus came to Galilee proclaiming good news and inviting people to believe in this good news.

Mark did not invent the word *evangelion*: It is found in ancient Greek literature as a technical term for a message of victory, or other message that brought joy. Mark (and earlier Paul) adopted this word to describe the message of Jesus. It was an apt term. God was doing something new in Jesus Christ, so a report on it was newsworthy. God was doing something very good for us through Jesus, so the report was not only news but good news. It was a message of victory, Jesus' victory over sin and death; it was a message that should bring joy to everyone who heard it. On every count it was appropriate for Mark to begin his book with the words, "The beginning of the good news of Jesus Christ" (NRSV). It was so appropriate that his book would eventually simply be called *good news* — or a *gospel*.

Jesus' first words in the Gospel of Mark are likewise concerned with good news: "This is the time of fulfillment. The kingdom of God is at hand. Repent, and believe in the gospel" (Mk 1:15). The good news that Jesus brought was that the moment had arrived for the reign of God to be established. For long centuries, sin and suffering and death had reigned over the earth. Now God was acting through Jesus to conquer sin and suffering and death. God's reign was becoming present in the person of Jesus, through his teachings and healings and exorcisms: "If it is by the Spirit of God that I drive out demons, then the kingdom of God has come among you" (Mt 12:28). That's good news! That's a message of victory that should bring us joy.

Yet two thousand years later, there is still sin and suffering and death. The reign of God has begun among us, but it has not yet reached its fulfillment. Jesus taught that he would return in power to establish the definitive reign of God. He asked us to pray for this to happen, for that is really what we are asking for when we pray the prayer that Jesus taught us: "Father in heaven, glorify your name, establish your reign, carry out your will." Jesus assured us that our prayers would be heard (see Mt 6:7-10; Lk 11:2-13). This is good news for us: Jesus will complete his work, so there is hope for the world and hope for us.

Do we fully accept this good news, this message of Jesus' victory? Or has this news grown stale in our ears? Has it lost its element of being good news for us: Does it no longer bring us joy? Perhaps we need to adjust our thinking. Jesus' invitation, "Repent and believe in the good news," could be translated, "Change your mind and believe in the good news." The Greek word for repentance (*metanoia*) literally means a change of mind. Changed behavior should result from a change of mind, but true repentance begins in the mind and heart.

Jesus' invitation could be paraphrased: Change your thinking and accept that the Gospel message is really good news. Change the way you look at this world; perceive the signs of God's reign. Change your expectations for what lies ahead, and live in hope. Believe what I tell you, for it is the best possible news for you.

The Persistent Sower

"A farmer went out to sow his seed. As he was scattering the seed, some fell along the path, and the birds came and ate it up. Some fell on rocky places, where it did not have much soil. It sprang up quickly, because the soil was shallow. But when the sun came up, the plants were scorched, and they withered because they had no root. Other seed fell among thorns, which grew up and choked the plants, so they did not bear grain. Still other seed fell on good soil. It came up, grew and produced a crop, multiplying thirty, sixty, or even a hundred times" (Mk 4:3-8 NIV).

The first reaction of those who have seen Kansas wheat fields to this parable of Jesus might be, "That's pretty sloppy sowing. Why didn't the farmer just sow on rich soil and skip the rest?"

But the rocky rolling hills of Galilee are not the flat fertile fields of Kansas. Topsoil is patchy and thin in many places around Nazareth, Cana, and Capernaum. Farmers in the time of Jesus could either scatter their seed on the land that was available to them, or not sow at all. A farmer who demanded a field of rich soil before sowing, a field free of rocks, weeds, and paths, would have been better advised to take up fishing for a living.

There were, to be sure, some excellent fields in a few of the valleys, but prized land, then as now, tended to belong to the wealthy. Ordinary folks generally had to make do with rocky soil. When Jesus told this parable to ordinary people, they knew from experience what he was talking about.

In Jesus' interpretation of this parable, the seed is the word of God (see Mk 4:14; Lk 8:11). This makes for a paradox. Elsewhere in Scripture the word of God is described as "living and active. Sharper than any double-edged sword" (Heb 4:12 NIV). It is said to be like fire, or "like a hammer that breaks a rock" (Jer 23:29 NIV). The word of God is portrayed as never returning to God void but always accomplishing his will and achieving the end for which he spoke it (see Is 55:10-11).

Yet in Jesus' parable, some of the seed is sown in vain; in his interpretation, this means that God's word may be spoken in vain. Sometimes God's word is snatched away by Satan; sometimes it is initially welcomed but then forgotten in a time of difficulty; sometimes the life that springs forth from God's word is choked out by the distractions of the world before it can bear fruit (see Mk 4:15-19). Whatever the inner power of God's word, the soil on which it is sown still plays a role in determining its fruitfulness.

If God wanted to make sure that he never wasted his breath, he could speak only to those who would respond wholeheart-edly and persevere and become saints. He could sow only in Kansas and not in Galilee, as it were. But that is not the course he has chosen to follow. God is a "sloppy sower," scattering his word widely, speaking it even to those who may make an imperfect response.

The parable of the sower and the seed is one more indication that God is rather indiscriminate in his love. "He causes his sun to rise on the evil and the good, and sends rain on the righteous and the unrighteous" (Mt 5:45 NIV), thereby providing them with food. He is "kind to the ungrateful and wicked" (Lk 6:35 NIV), and not merely to those who revere him.

He scatters his saving word like a Galilean farmer sowing his rocky plot, hoping for a hundredfold return, but knowing that it will often be much less.

That is good news for us who have many patches of rocky soil in our lives. That is good news for us who have never made even a thirtyfold response to God's word, while we see others around us bearing a hundredfold harvest. That is good news for us who are still struggling with assaults from Satan, who find that we have little strength in times of difficulty, who worry that the word that we have heard is being snuffed out by all the cares and distractions of our lives. God persists in sowing his word even in Galilee, even on rocky soil, even in us.

Do You Want to Be Well?

Now there is in Jerusalem at the Sheep [Gate] a
pool called in Hebrew Bethesda, with five porticoes.
In these lay a large number of ill, blind, lame, and
crippled. One man was there who had been ill for
thirty-eight years. When Jesus saw him lying there
and knew that he had been ill for a long time, he
said to him, "Do you want to be well?" The sick
man answered him, "Sir, I have no one to put me
into the pool when the water is stirred up; while I
am on my way, someone else gets down there before
me" (Jn 5:2-7).

Jesus asked this man a straightforward question, easily answered yes or no: "Do you want to be well?" But instead of giving Jesus a straightforward reply, the man gave an excuse for why he was crippled. Rather than tell Jesus, "Yes, I want to be well," he tried to justify his infirmity.

If this man had no expectation of being healed, why did he come to the pool of Bethesda?

Perhaps it was pleasant to pass the day in the shade of the porticoes, talking to others with debilitating afflictions. Perhaps it allowed him to tell himself, "I am doing all I can to get well: I am lying by the pool — even though I know I won't be healed." After thirty-eight years, he had not only been crippled most all his life, but being crippled had become his way of life.

We may have a similar attitude toward our spiritual infirmities.

Some of our sins may have been with us so long that they

are part of our way of life; some of our character faults may be so deeply rooted in our makeup that they have become part of our identity. We may have come to accept ourselves as spiritually crippled; we may have decided that that is simply the way we are.

Oh, we might still be making efforts to rid ourselves of these sins and faults, but our efforts may have become duplicitous: We try knowing that we will fail; we try only so that we can tell God on judgment day, "I tried." We harbor no more hope of getting spiritually well than the man by the pool had of getting into the water in time.

Jesus confronts us with the same question he asked the man who was crippled: "Do you want to be well?" Never mind the excuses you have for being the way you are; never mind the list of efforts you have made — do you want to be well?

Do you want to be freed from your sins, addictions, and chronic faults? Or are you so comfortable with your old self, so used to lying in the shade and justifying your condition, that you really do not want to get well?

Fortunately for the crippled man, Jesus healed him anyway: "Jesus said to him, 'Rise, take up your mat, and walk.' Immediately the man became well, took up his mat, and walked" (Jn 5:8-9). The man had made no act of faith in Jesus (he didn't even know who Jesus was — see Jn 5:13), nor had he asked to be healed. But nevertheless, Jesus healed him by the pool of Bethesda. The name of this pool is a clue to why Jesus did so: Bethesda means *house of (divine) mercy*. Jesus healed out of mercy; Jesus demonstrated that God is merciful to us even though we do not deserve his mercy.

It is because of God's mercy shown in Jesus that we can face up to the question, "Do you want to be well?" We can respond, "Lord, heal me of my sins even if I cling to them; free me from my addictions and faults; raise me from the paralysis of my old self. In your mercy, raise me up now to walk with you as your disciple; raise me up on the last day to eternal life."

Who Can Be Saved?

Jesus looked around and said to his disciples, "How hard it is for those who have wealth to enter the kingdom of God!" The disciples were amazed at his words. So Jesus again said to them in reply, "Children, how hard it is to enter the kingdom of God! It is easier for a camel to pass through [the] eye of [a] needle than for one who is rich to enter the kingdom of God." They were exceedingly astonished and said among themselves, "Then who can be saved?" Jesus looked at them and said, "For human beings it is impossible, but not for God. All things are possible for God" (Mk 10:23-27).

While the disciples were not destitute, neither were they wealthy. Archaeologists have discovered Peter's house in Capernaum, and it is what one might expect to find as the home of a first-century fisherman. Its single room with courtyard would be considered Third World housing today. Most of the other followers of Jesus came from similar economic backgrounds.

Why, then, were the disciples "amazed" and "exceedingly astonished" when Jesus insisted that it was hard for those with wealth to enter the kingdom of God? If we had been in their shoes, our reaction might have been, "We're not wealthy; Jesus' warning doesn't apply to us."

But that was not the reaction of Jesus' first disciples: They reacted as if Jesus' words threatened their own salvation. "Then who can be saved?" was a way of asking, "Then how can we be saved?"

Why did the disciples react in this manner? I believe it was because they understood wealth as a sign of God's favor. Did not God promise prosperity to those who obeyed his commands (see Dt 28:1-14)? Did he not promise success to the upright (see Ps 1:3)? Did not God show his favor for people like Solomon by giving them great wealth (see 1 Kgs 3:13; 10:14-29)? If wealth was a sign of God's favor, then the wealthy should have had the best chance of entering his kingdom.

This was not what Jesus was trying to teach his followers about wealth. He taught that wealth was not a sign that one was on the way to salvation, but a potential obstacle to salvation. Wealth was too often the fruit of serving mammon rather than God. Jesus had quite a bit to say about the dangers and proper use of money, and he placed special emphasis on helping the poor. He had just asked a rich man to sell what he owned and give the proceeds to the poor if he wished to be a disciple and have treasure in heaven (see Mk 10:21).

I do not think that the disciples grasped Jesus' message yet; they still looked on wealth as a sign of God's favor. Hence their amazement at Jesus' words really boiled down to wondering, "If God's apparent favorites won't be saved, who will be? If those that God has blessed in this life won't enter the kingdom, then what hope is there for us?"

In response to their puzzlement, Jesus did not immediately try to correct their misunderstanding of wealth as a sign of God's favor, but instead tried to steer the conversation to a deeper level. No economic or social or religious status, no human achievement, nothing at all can pry open the door of heaven save God opening it to welcome us in.

Salvation is a gift from God. It is utterly impossible for us to save ourselves, because salvation is essentially union with God, and union with God is beyond the capabilities of human nature. Only God can transform and elevate us to make such union possible. With God all things are possible — even lifting up our lowly flesh into resurrected eternal life.

Of course God is interested in how we behave. That is why

Jesus reminded the rich man of the commandments (see Mk 10:19) and invited him to give what he owned to the poor (see Mk 10:21). That is why we must be on guard against obstacles to our salvation — such as wealth which puffs us up into camels nosing the eye of a needle. But our salvation fundamentally comes from the grace of God, for our salvation is a matter of us attaining the impossible.

Who can be saved? Those for whom God does the impossible.

The Good Shepherd

"I am the good shepherd.

"My sheep listen to my voice; I know them and they follow me. I give them eternal life, and they shall never perish; no one can snatch them out of my hand. My Father, who has given them to me, is greater than all; no one can snatch them out of my Father's hand" (Jn 10:11, 27-29 NIV).

Jesus tells us that he is the good shepherd, and he refers to us as sheep. No doubt his first audience was a lot more familiar with sheep than we are and found immediate meaning in his words. But what are we to learn from them?

Perhaps a good starting point is the parable of the one lost sheep in chapter fifteen of Luke's Gospel. When this single animal wanders away from the flock, the shepherd leaves his other ninety-nine sheep and goes looking for it until he finds it. Jesus clearly intends this parable as a teaching about God's love for us and his readiness to forgive us; in the same chapter of Luke is found the parable of the prodigal son.

What is noteworthy is that the shepherd does not wait for the lost sheep to discover that it is lost and return to the flock. Rather the shepherd goes out of his way to go after the stray, even though the man already has ninety-nine other sheep to occupy his concern.

Our understanding of repentance is usually slightly different. We tend to think that when we sin God sits back and waits patiently for us to come to our senses and return to him, begging forgiveness. But that is not how Jesus portrays this shepherd. He tells us that the shepherd searches out the lost sheep, searching until he has found it and brought it back to the flock.

That is the kind of shepherd Jesus is. He does not merely wait for us to come back to him; he takes the initiative to come after us when we have strayed. The work of reconciliation is not left entirely to us.

Jesus also says that no one shall snatch his sheep away from him. We can sometimes think of our lives as a gigantic struggle, with Jesus beckoning on one side and various forces of temptation and evil pulling us the other way. Jesus assures us that we are not going to be swept away as hapless victims of these forces. He has a claim on us and is not going to relinquish us.

We can certainly turn our backs on Jesus and reject him; he does not take away our free will. But he is not going to stand idly by while forces of evil overpower us. The power of Jesus is greater than the forces that oppose him — because the power of Jesus is the power of God himself, and "no one can snatch them out of my hand" (Jn 10:28 NIV).

Jesus' determination to save us and give us eternal life is very good news for us. It is such good news that we might have trouble completely believing in it, conditioned as we are to doubt all the claims that are too good to be true.

But Jesus gives us incontrovertible evidence of the truth of his teaching about God's mercy toward us. He tells us that like the good shepherd he lays down his life for his sheep. His death to redeem us is the proof of how serious he is to save us and to reclaim us when we are lost. "But God demonstrates his own love for us in this: While we were still sinners, Christ died for us" (Rom 5:8 NIV) and now Christ "is at the right hand of God and is also interceding for us" (Rom 8:34 NIV).

Could Jesus have done anything more to prove his love for us and his determination that we not be lost? If he was willing to die for us, would he not be willing to search us out when we stray? If he has already given up his life for us so that we might have eternal life, will he not now do all in his power to preserve eternal life in us?

Living Water

On the last and greatest day of the Feast, Jesus stood and said in a loud voice, "If anyone is thirsty, let him come to me and drink. Whoever believes in me, as the Scripture has said, streams of living water will flow from within him." By this he meant the Spirit, whom those who believed in him were later to receive (Jn 7:37-39 NIV).

The setting was the temple in Jerusalem, during the feast of Tabernacles. On each of the seven days of the feast, water was drawn from the Gihon Spring, lying southeast of the temple in the Kidron Valley. This water was carried in procession into the temple and poured over the altar. On the last day, when the celebration reached its climax, Jesus stood up in the temple precincts and proclaimed himself the true source of living water — a proclamation that John sees as the fulfillment of Old Testament prophecy.

But to what prophecy is John referring here? No Old Testament prophecy exactly matches the words John uses, but several convey the essential thought. One important passage for understanding the significance of Jesus' action is from the prophet Ezekiel (see Ez 47:1-12).

Ezekiel sees a vision of a spring gushing forth from the Holy of Holies, flowing past the altar, out of the temple, and into the Kidron Valley. As it flows through the valley it grows from a shallow brook only ankle deep to a stream waist deep, then finally becomes a mighty river impossible to cross. Everywhere this river flows trees spring to life along its banks, and "every month they shall bear fresh fruit, for they shall be watered by the flow from the sanctuary" (Ez 47:12). Not only is the fruit good to eat, but the leaves of the trees cure illness. Finally the river empties into the Dead Sea, making its brackish water wholesome. Fish begin to live in the sea, as plentifully as in the Mediterranean (see Ez 47:10).

This is a remarkable vision in itself. Normally a spring is strongest and purest at its mouth, and the farther its water flows the more it evaporates or is absorbed into the ground. But the living water in Ezekiel's vision grows mightier as it flows.

Further, the countryside between Jerusalem and the Dead Sea is a desolate wasteland, rocky and incapable of sustaining life. But as this stream flows through it life springs forth, life that no normal water could sustain.

Finally, when the stream reaches the Dead Sea it transforms it. This contrasts with the River Jordan, whose waters are pure but become polluted as soon as they empty into the Dead Sea.

When Ezekiel proclaimed this vision it was a message of the power of God. God's grace brings life to what is barren, even as this stream that flowed from the temple brought life wherever it went. God's grace overcomes seemingly insurmountable obstacles, even as this stream conquered the desolation of the Judean wilderness and the poisonous salts of the Dead Sea.

This prophecy of Ezekiel was one of the passages read during the feast of Tabernacles. When Jesus stood up and cried out, he was proclaiming that he was the source of the living water that Ezekiel had foretold. He was the new temple (see Jn 2:19-21), from which would flow the living water of eternal life that he had promised to the woman at the well (see Jn 4:10-14). From him would issue a mighty, growing stream, bringing salvation wherever it went. John adds that Jesus was speaking of the Spirit, whom all who believed in Jesus were to receive.

Ezekiel's vision of the stream helps us understand something of the work and power of the Spirit. To be touched by the

Spirit is to be transformed. No matter how barren we are in ourselves, the Spirit can bring us to life. No matter how overwhelming our difficulties may appear, the Spirit has the power to overcome them.

When a visitor to the Holy Land follows the Kidron Valley down to the Dead Sea, the desolation of the area is overwhelming, and it appears that nothing could ever grow there. It seems impossible that fish could ever survive in the lifeless waters of the Dead Sea. Yet the living water that issues forth from Jesus can bring life to even more desolate areas of our soul. The Holy Spirit whom he has given can transform us and give us abundant life.

God's Standard

"I tell you, unless your righteousness surpasses that of the scribes and Pharisees, you will not enter into the kingdom of heaven" (Mt 5:20).

Any Pharisees in the crowd gathered to listen to Jesus' Sermon on the Mount must have found these words upsetting.

Consider what it meant to be a Pharisee. They believed obedience to God's laws to be the most important thing in life. They regarded the law so highly that they studied it constantly; they considered obedience so important that they surrounded the law with numerous regulations to insure perfect fidelity to it. It was not easy to be a conscientious Pharisee.

Unfortunately there were intrinsic hazards to their approach to pleasing God. Some of them were tempted to look down on those who had not studied the law or were lax about obeying it: "This rabble knows nothing about the Law — they are damned" (Jn 7:49 JB). They could get so wrapped up in the details of regulations that they lost sight of their purpose; they could pay their tithe on kitchen spices while neglecting justice and mercy (see Mt 23:23).

But such failings did not infect every Pharisee. Nor should we understand that such failings were the central concern of Jesus' words. Jesus was not here condemning hypocrisy. Rather, the context indicates that Jesus' meaning was closer to: "Unless you live by standards that are even *higher* than the exacting standards Pharisees live by, you will fall short of entering the kingdom of God." That would have been an upsetting statement for any devout Pharisee to hear, since it told him that all his painstaking efforts were doomed to ultimate failure.

Understood in this way, these words of Jesus should also upset us. We are not Pharisees, but we are tempted to follow the Pharisees' path to salvation. We are tempted to believe that if we succeed in obeying a certain code of laws we will have succeeded in pleasing God and earning heaven. Our understanding of God's law for us is probably a good deal more permissive than the laws and regulations a Pharisee tried to follow, but that isn't the issue.

Jesus, in the Sermon on the Mount, did not try to improve on the code of the Pharisees by tightening it up here and there. He rather set forth a standard of conduct that far transcended the code of the Pharisees, and far transcends the standards we expect of ourselves.

Jesus tells us that God's requirements of us are much higher than we think. They are in fact impossibly high: "So be perfect, just as your heavenly Father is perfect" (Mt 5:48). We are commanded to love one another with the perfect love that God demonstrated for us in Jesus Christ: "I give you a new commandment: love one another. As I have loved you, so you also should love one another" (Jn 13:34). Note that Jesus does not put this forward as a suggestion but as a commandment. Similarly the holiness that is expected of us is not just an ideal but an entrance requirement to heaven.

Our response must be like that of the disciples on another occasion, when Jesus made it quite clear that God expected much more than they had anticipated. "They were exceedingly astonished and said among themselves, "Then who can be saved?" Jesus looked at them and said, "For human beings it is impossible, but not for God. All things are possible for God" (Mk 10:26-27 JB). We have to rely on God to accomplish in us something that is far beyond our ability to accomplish ourselves: to make us holy and pleasing to himself, to transform us so that we are capable of living according to his standards. That means that we have to rely on the grace of God for our salvation, not on our own achievements, even if we are as scrupulous about our conduct as a conscientious Pharisee. That means that despite all our efforts, as necessary as they are, salvation is a gift.

God's Double Standard

"But love your enemies, do good to them, and lend to them without expecting to get anything back. Then your reward will be great, and you will be sons of the Most High, because he is kind to the ungrateful and wicked. Be merciful, just as your Father is merciful.

"Do not judge, and you will not be judged. Do not condemn, and you will not be condemned. Forgive, and you will be forgiven. Give, and it will be given to you. A good measure, pressed down, shaken together and running over, will be poured into your lap. For with the measure you use, it will be measured to you" (Lk 6:35-38 NIV).

What is God's standard for how he deals with us? The words of Jesus from the Gospel of Luke suggest that God operates by two different standards.

One standard is the standard of strict justice or reciprocity; as we do, so God will do to us, both positively and negatively. On the positive side, if we give, God will give to us, and if we pardon, God will pardon us. On the negative side, if we do not judge or condemn, then we will not be judged or condemned. According to the standard of justice, the measure we use in our dealings with others or with God will be the measure he uses in dealing with us.

Jesus accents the positive side of this standard, emphasizing that in return for our goodness we will receive "a good measure, pressed down, shaken together and running over."

The image is of grain being measured out generously and given to us. Jesus here says nothing about our selfishness resulting in a niggardly measure being given back to us by God, although the standard of reciprocity would logically demand this. In his use of this image, Jesus does not threaten punishment for evil behavior so much as promise abundant reward for good behavior.

Jesus also speaks of God operating by a second standard, a standard of compassion. By the standard of compassion, God is good to the wicked, even though they deserve his wrath. By this standard, God gives good things even to those who show no gratitude for his gifts. By this standard, God loves even his enemies. Jesus asks his disciples to imitate God's standard of compassion: to return good for evil, to lend without hope of repayment, to answer curses with blessings. Jesus can only ask his followers to behave in this way because this is the standard that God follows in his dealings with them.

It appears, then, that God operates by a double standard. On the one hand, he promises to reward us if we live as he invites us to live. He promises to forgive us if we forgive others; he promises to bless us if we love our enemies; he promises that he will always exceed our measure of generosity to us. But on the other hand, God is described by Jesus as being good to the ungrateful and the wicked, as sending his rain both on the just and the unjust, as loving even those who are his enemies. Strict justice would demand that God should act otherwise: He should punish the wicked instead of loving them, he should only send his blessings on those who deserve them, he should strike down his enemies and stifle those who curse him.

It would be dangerous for us to persist in our sins because we presume on God's mercy; it would be foolhardy for us to believe that God will never call us to account for how we have lived. There is much in the Bible that speaks about God's judgment. Yet it does seem that God has stacked the deck in our favor. If we do good, he promises to reward us; if we fall into sin, he offers us forgiveness. If we love him, he promises to overwhelm us with his love; if we are cold or indifferent to him, he tries to woo us to himself.

By the double standard of God, his Son Jesus came to gather to himself all who turned to him — and to die on the cross even for those who rejected him and put him to death. Jesus taught us to love our enemies because that is what his Father does; Jesus demonstrated love of enemies from the cross as he prayed, "Father, forgive them" (Lk 23:34 NIV).

> The Lord is compassionate and gracious,
> slow to anger, abounding in love.
> He will not always accuse,
> nor will he harbor his anger forever;
> he does not treat us as our sins deserve
> or repay us according to our iniquities.
> For as high as the heavens are above the
>   earth,
> so great is his love for those who fear
>   him (Ps 103:8-11 NIV).

God's Compassion

"Therefore, the kingdom of heaven is like a king who wanted to settle accounts with his servants. As he began the settlement, a man who owed him ten thousand talents was brought to him. Since he was not able to pay, the master ordered that he and his wife and his children and all that he had be sold to repay the debt.

"The servant fell on his knees before him. 'Be patient with me,' he begged, 'and I will pay back everything.' The servant's master took pity on him, canceled the debt and let him go" (Mt 18:23-27 NIV).

To drive home his teaching on forgiveness, Jesus told a parable about a servant who had been forgiven much but then refused to forgive a little (see Mt 18:23-35). This parable is a drama in several acts, and its first scene can be read as a parable in itself.

The servant owed his master "ten thousand talents" — an amount one reference work explains as "at least two hundred four metric tons of silver." This would represent something like two hundred thousand years' wages for an ordinary worker at the time of Jesus. The servant therefore owed a truly immense sum, far more than he could ever work off. His promise, "I will pay back everything" was ridiculous: It was impossible for him to repay what he owed.

But note what happened: "The servant's master took pity on him, canceled the debt and let him go." His master granted him complete forgiveness, giving him a fresh start.

That is probably not how you or I would have handled it. If someone owed us more money than they had, we might say, "Pay what you can, even if you can't pay the full amount." Or,

"Take some time to get your affairs in order, and then begin making payments." We would keep the debtor in debt to us so we could salvage as much as possible of what was owed us. Our least likely response would be, "I completely forgive your debt." Yet the master in this parable made just this response — and Jesus says that this is what God is like. The reign of heaven begins with God extending forgiveness to those who owe him far more than they could ever repay. Moved with compassion, God wipes away our debts of sin, however great.

So goes Act One of this parable. Jesus presented this scene to prepare the way for the point of the parable: Since we have been forgiven by God, we should forgive others. No matter how much we may have to forgive, it will never come anywhere near matching the great amount that we have been forgiven. It is not that God has fixed a parking ticket for us, and now we have to forgive someone who has wrecked our new car. It's rather that God has forgiven us billions, and we in turn need to pick up the lunch tab for others now and then.

The point of the whole parable should not be lost. But neither should the point of Act One. The reign of God begins with God having compassion on us and extending great forgiveness to us. God has first loved us; God has acted first to draw us to himself. We need to be concerned about the response we make to him, but we should never lose sight of the fact that it is a response, a reaction — something we do because of what God has already done.

Most of us need a periodic reminder that our salvation begins with God: that he has acted first out of compassion for us, that he has loved us when we were not very lovable, that the magnitude of his compassionate love far overshadows anything we could ever do for him. As John writes, "This is love: not that we loved God, but that he loved us and sent his Son as an atoning sacrifice for our sins" (1 Jn 4:10 NIV). John, like Jesus' parable, draws out the implication of God's love for us: "Since God so loved us, we also ought to love one another" (1 Jn 4:11 NIV). But everything starts with God's love, with God acting first in immense compassion.

Life From Death

Jesus wept.

Then the Jews said, "See how he loved him!"

Jesus, once more deeply moved, came to the tomb. It was a cave with a stone laid across the entrance. "Take away the stone," he said.

"But Lord," said Martha, the sister of the dead man, "by this time there is a bad odor, for he has been there four days."

Then Jesus said, "Did I not tell you that if you believed, you would see the glory of God?"

So they took away the stone. Then Jesus looked up and said, "Father, I thank you that you heard me."

When he had said this, Jesus called in a loud voice, "Lazarus, come out!" (Jn 11:35-36, 38-41, 43 NIV).

The Gospels present us with three incidents in which Jesus raises someone from the dead: the daughter of Jairus (see Mk 5:21-24, 35-43), the son of the widow of Naim (see Lk 7:11-16), and Lazarus of Bethany, brother of Mary and Martha (see Jn 11:1-44). Since our ultimate hope in Jesus is that he will also raise us from our graves, it is worth reflecting on what these incidents teach us.

One noteworthy feature of these three incidents is the compassion of Jesus. He went to Jairus's house in response to his plea on behalf of his daughter (see Mk 5:23-24). He didn't even wait to be asked to do something for the only son of the widow of Naim: When Jesus saw the funeral procession, "his heart went out to her and he said, 'Don't cry.' " (Lk 7:13 NIV). Mary and Martha sent a message to Jesus, "Lord, the one you love is sick" (Jn 11:3 NIV). His love for Lazarus was obvious to everyone who saw him at the tomb (see Jn 11:36).

If we were to ask what Lazarus and the daughter of Jairus and the son of the widow did to deserve being raised from the dead, we would be hard pressed to come up with much. There is no indication that Jesus ever met Jairus's daughter before he restored her to life; he simply responded to her father's request. Likewise, there is no indication that he had previously known the mother and son of Naim; Jesus, rather, acted out of spontaneous compassion. With Lazarus, the case is slightly different: Lazarus and his sisters were close friends of Jesus; he ate with them (see Jn 12:1-3) and probably stayed in their home in Bethany on the Mount of Olives when he was preaching in Jerusalem (see Mt 21:17; Lk 21:37).

The three who were raised do nothing in the Gospel narratives before being brought back to life: They basically appear on the scene in each account already dead. Scripture says nothing to indicate that these three people particularly deserved what must be regarded as the greatest of miracles, to be brought back to life after having died.

That very fact holds out great hope for us. What we look forward to in Christ Jesus — resurrection to eternal life — is something humanly impossible to achieve. It is beyond the capability of medical science to restore life to someone who is corrupting in the tomb. How much more impossible it is for us to give ourselves unending life in glorified bodies! Nor is this something we can really earn. Even if we behave very well in this life, even if we obey God's laws perfectly, eternal life is not something we are capable of earning as our due.

By clumsy analogy we might imagine ourselves owning a particularly nice pet mouse: No matter how well-behaved it was, it could never earn the right to be changed into a human being. So, too, we can never earn what we hope to receive: resurrection in Christ Jesus to eternal life. It is something that we will be given, not that we will merit, no matter how good we are.

This truth is symbolized in the three Gospel incidents we have been examining. In every case Jesus raises the dead person out of compassion. In no case is it something that the dead person earned or was due. The most the dead person could have done was to have been a friend of Jesus during his or her lifetime, and asked to receive new life from him, and perhaps had others ask on his or her behalf. Beyond that, life from death is something that Jesus freely gives us — but also eagerly gives, because he is the compassion of God come among us. God gives us life because he loves us, and for no other reason.

Of course, Jesus wants his friends to respect and obey his Father's laws. But we should not confuse the obedience we owe God with earning the risen and eternal life he wants to give us. As St. Paul so strongly emphasized, eternal life is God's gift to us.

3

The Friends of Jesus

As they continued their journey he entered a village where a woman whose name was Martha welcomed him. She had a sister named Mary [who] sat beside the Lord at his feet listening to him speak (Lk 10:38-39).

The Eyes of Simeon

Now there was a man in Jerusalem called Simeon, who was righteous and devout. He was waiting for the consolation of Israel, and the Holy Spirit was upon him. It had been revealed to him by the Holy Spirit that he would not die before he had seen the Lord's Christ. Moved by the Spirit, he went into the temple courts. When the parents brought in the child Jesus to do for him what the custom of the Law required, Simeon took him in his arms and praised God, saying:

"Sovereign Lord, as you have promised,
you now dismiss your servant in peace.
For my eyes have seen your salvation,
which you have prepared in the sight of all people,
a light for revelation to the Gentiles
and for glory to your people Israel" (Lk 2:25-32 NIV).

The Gospels paint a picture of Jesus' disciples being very slow to understand him and his mission. Repeatedly they must ask what a parable means, or they miss the point of his teaching (see Mk 4:10, 40-41; 8:15-21, 32; 9:32-34; 10:37-38). Luke uses repetition to emphasize their lack of comprehension: "But they did not understand what this meant. It was hidden from them, so that they did not grasp it, and they were afraid to ask him about it" (Lk 9:45 NIV; see also 18:34).

Simeon's insight into the infant he holds in his arms stands in stark contrast to the later incomprehension of the disciples. Simeon gazed on Jesus and saw the fulfillment of God's plan of salvation for the world. Many others who were in the temple that day glanced at Jesus in the arms of Mary and saw only a small baby. The overwhelming number of those who saw Jesus throughout his years on earth failed to see what Simeon saw.

Simeon saw what he saw because of the Holy Spirit. Again, Luke uses repetition for emphasis: The Holy Spirit was upon him; the Holy Spirit had revealed to him that he would see the Messiah; the Holy Spirit had brought him to the temple that day (see Lk 2:25-27).

What did Simeon see? Simeon proclaimed Jesus to be "glory to your people Israel" (Lk 2:32 NIV). John also saw this glory: "The Word became flesh and made his dwelling among us. We have seen his glory, the glory of the One and Only, who came from the Father, full of grace and truth (Jn 1:14 NIV). But this glory was not readily apparent to everyone who passed Jesus on the street: Most of those who lived for years with Jesus in Nazareth failed to see his glory (see Mk 6:1-3). It took the inspiration of the Holy Spirit for Simeon and John to see that Jesus was the glory of God among us, come to bring glory to his people.

Simeon also proclaimed the infant Jesus to be "a light for revelation to the Gentiles" (Lk 2:32 NIV). Even after Jesus' resurrection it was not easy for the Church to grasp this truth. The question of whether Gentiles could be admitted to the Church, and under what conditions, was the source of much debate, and provides the underlying drama of the first half of the Acts of the Apostles. Paul must spend a good amount of ink wrestling with this question — and yet here is Simeon, holding the infant Jesus in his arms and seeing that this child will be the means of salvation for Gentiles as well as Jews.

Clearly the Holy Spirit gave Simeon great prophetic insight, a moment of great clarity about Jesus.

We too need to have the Holy Spirit inspire and enlighten

us, just as he inspired and enlightened Simeon. Even though we follow Jesus, we, like his first followers, may be missing part of his message. Even though we acknowledge Jesus as Savior and Lord, we may be like those in the early Church who failed to grasp the full implications of the lordship of Jesus, the full scope of God's plan of salvation for the world.

We each need our moments of clarity in which the Holy Spirit makes plain to us what it means that Jesus is the Savior of the world and our Savior, what it means for us to be his disciples, what it takes to model our lives on his. We each need the Holy Spirit to open our eyes to see what Simeon saw.

Tax Collectors

As Jesus passed on from there, he saw a man named Matthew sitting at the customs post. He said to him, "Follow me." And he got up and followed him. While he was at table in his house, many tax collectors and sinners came and sat with Jesus and his disciples. The Pharisees saw this and said to his disciples, "Why does your teacher eat with tax collectors and sinners?" (Mt 9:9-11).

Tax collectors were an object of scorn at the time of Jesus, spoken of in the same breath with sinners. Even granting that no one likes to pay taxes, why were tax collectors so despised?

There were several factors.

First, Jewish tax collectors were agents, directly or indirectly, of Rome. Rome had conquered the Holy Land in 63 B.C., and imposed taxes. Every tax payment reminded Jews that they were under Roman rule, and they despised those who collected taxes on behalf of Rome.

Second, the tax system lent itself to abuse. One arrangement was to auction off the right to collect taxes to the highest bidder, and then allow the tax collector to keep anything he could collect over that amount. It was a green light for greed, and many tax collectors took full advantage of it. Hence, John the Baptist admonished tax collectors, "Stop collecting more than what is prescribed" (Lk 3:13).

As a result of these factors, tax collectors were considered unscrupulous extortionists working for a foreign power.

Matthew is described as "sitting at the customs post" (Mt 9:9) outside Capernaum. A duty was imposed on merchandise at border crossings. Herod Philip governed the territory east of the Jordan River and Herod Antipas governed the territory to the west, both ruling as clients of Rome. Capernaum had a customs post because it lay on a trade route from Damascus, and it was the first town on this route west of the Jordan River.

Matthew was an agent of Herod Antipas, collecting duties on merchandise entering his realm. Working for Herod Antipas would have been another mark against Matthew: This was the Herod Antipas who had married his brother's wife, executed John the Baptist, and wanted to kill Jesus.

It is little wonder then that those attending a dinner with Matthew are described as "tax collectors and sinners": They were probably the only people willing to accept an invitation to eat at his house.

Except for Jesus.

Jesus was not ashamed to associate with tax collectors and other outcasts. That was the charge against Jesus: "He is . . . a friend of tax collectors and sinners" (Mt 11:19).

Why didn't hanging around with tax collectors bother Jesus?

For one thing, Jesus had nothing against paying taxes to Rome: "Then repay to Caesar what belongs to Caesar and to God what belongs to God" (Mt 22:21). Jesus came to inaugurate the kingdom of God, not to replace Roman rule by Jewish rule.

For another thing, Jesus recognized that there could be honorable people in unesteemed occupations. Zacchaeus was such a person: a "chief tax collector" (Lk 19:2) who gave half of his income to the poor and made fourfold restitution to anyone he defrauded (Luke 19:8 is best translated in the present tense as an indication of what Zacchaeus was already doing).

But most importantly, Jesus came to bring salvation to everyone, tax collectors as well as fishermen. He no more held himself aloof from sinners than a doctor avoided sick people: "Those who are well do not need a physician, but the sick do.

Go and learn the meaning of the words, 'I desire mercy, not sacrifice' " (Mt 9:12-13).

There is both comfort and challenge for us in the example of Jesus. He does not hold himself aloof from us, no matter who we are. But he asks us to likewise go out to the outcasts, recognizing the goodness that is in them, and bringing them the mercy and message of Jesus.

The Twelve

In those days he departed to the mountain to pray, and he spent the night in prayer to God. When day came, he called his disciples to himself, and from them he chose Twelve, whom he also named apostles: Simon, whom he named Peter, and his brother Andrew, James, John, Philip, Bartholomew, Matthew, Thomas, James the son of Alphaeus, Simon who was called a Zealot, and Judas the son of James, and Judas Iscariot, who became a traitor (Lk 6:12-16).

What went through the minds of the Twelve when Jesus called them forth to be his apostles? Perhaps awe that they were chosen, perhaps excitement over what lay ahead. And, perhaps, as well, some uneasiness as they glanced at who else had been chosen, and wondered, "Am I expected to get along with *these* people?"

Matthew was a tax collector (see Mt 10:3), an occupation that lent itself to corruption. Many devout Jews held themselves aloof from tax collectors as sinners (see Mk 2:16): Did some of the Twelve find Matthew's presence in their midst offensive?

Furthermore, Matthew was an agent of Herod Antipas, who ruled Galilee on behalf of Rome. Simon, "who was called a Zealot," probably harbored deep resentment of Roman agents: The Jewish rebellion against Rome in A.D. 66-70 would be led by Zealots. What did Simon the Zealot think of Matthew — and what did Matthew think of this Zealot?

James and John were known as "sons of thunder" (Mk 3:17); they were the ones who wanted to call down fire from heaven on a Samaritan village (see Lk 9:54). James and John jockeyed for positions of power and honor among the Twelve (see Mk 9:35-37), leading the other apostles to become indignant (see Mk 9:41). How easy was it to put up with these self-seeking "sons of thunder" day after day?

And what did the other eleven think of Judas Iscariot? He was the keeper of their common purse, but a thief (see Jn 12:6). How soon did the rest of the apostles catch on to his pilfering? What did this do to their relationship with him?

The Twelve seem a collection of people unlikely to get along very well with one another. Yet Jesus chose them after spending an entire night in prayer seeking his Father's will. Perhaps one lesson is this: Jesus doesn't choose his followers on the basis of their compatibility with one another. Rather, he chooses whom he chooses, and then teaches them how to behave as his disciples. If they carry out his teaching, then harmony can reign even in the most unlikely of groupings.

"Love your enemies," Jesus said (Mt 5:44). You there, Simon the Zealot, you must love Matthew the Roman agent — and you, Matthew, you must love Simon, who wants to put you out of business.

"If anyone wishes to be first, he shall be the last of all and the servant of all" (Mk 9:35). Did you hear that, James and John? And as for the rest of you: Are you indignant over James and John wanting places of honor because you want these honors for yourself?

"No one can serve God and wealth" (Lk 16:13 NRSV). Are you listening, Judas Iscariot?

"As I have loved you, so you also should love one another" (Jn 13:34). That was Jesus' command to all of them. He had loved those he had chosen, despite their faults, despite their many failures to understand him, despite however they might betray or deny him. They were to love one another with an equally resolute love.

If we chafe over the groupings in which we find ourselves — family or parish, neighborhood or work — then perhaps our chafing is a clue that we need to hear the words of Jesus more clearly and heed them more carefully. Perhaps Jesus chose Twelve who wouldn't naturally get along with one another so they could serve as an example for us, teaching us how to love those we are not naturally inclined to love.

Two Disciples

Then Mary took about a pint of pure nard, an expensive perfume; she poured it on Jesus' feet and wiped his feet with her hair. And the house was filled with the fragrance of the perfume.

But one of his disciples, Judas Iscariot, who was later to betray him, objected, "Why wasn't this perfume sold and the money given to the poor? It was worth a year's wages." He did not say this because he cared about the poor but because he was a thief; as keeper of the money bag, he used to help himself to what was put into it (Jn 12:3-6 NIV).

Each of the Gospels has a scene in which a woman anoints Jesus (see Mt 26:6-13; Mk 14:3-9; Lk 7:36-50; Jn 12:1-8). While it can be profitable to compare the different accounts, each should also be read and understood on its own.

In the Gospel of John, the woman who anoints Jesus is Mary of Bethany, the sister of Martha and Lazarus. Jesus interprets her anointing in terms of his coming burial (see Jn 12:7), but it is not clear that Mary was aware of this significance of her deed. She simply may have anointed his feet with perfumed oil as a gesture of love.

And what a gesture it was! The perfumed oil was worth a year's wages for an ordinary worker. There is no evidence that Mary, Martha, or Lazarus was wealthy; the Gospels present them as ordinary people. They are able to offer Jesus a meal when he visits, but it is a meal that Martha must prepare, indicating that they had no servants (see Lk 10:38-42).

It was, therefore, quite an extravagance for Mary to pour a year's wages worth of perfumed oil on Jesus' feet. Her act might have meant her using up her life's savings in one great gesture of love. We could compare it to a merchant finding a pearl of great price and selling everything in order to buy it — and then giving this pearl to Jesus.

Judas also plays a role in this incident. Whenever we think of Judas, we think of him as the one who betrayed Jesus. But he had not done so yet. When Mary anointed Jesus, Judas was still one of the Twelve who had been specially chosen by Jesus. He had even been entrusted with responsibility for the common fund that was used for expenses and helping the poor (see Jn 13:29). To an outside observer, Judas was not only one of the Twelve, but one of the leaders among the Twelve.

Tragically, he abused his position by stealing from the common fund. His words of concern for the poor were hypocritical: He simply wanted more money to flow into the common purse so that he could divert more into his own pocket. His greed would ultimately lead him to ask the enemies of Jesus, "What are you willing to give me if I hand him over to you?" (Mt 26:15 NIV).

What a contrast! One disciple gives to Jesus with reckless abandon; another disciple steals from Jesus and from the poor. One has no thought for herself, but only for the Jesus she loves. The other thinks only of himself, and of how he can use the position Jesus had given him for his own gain.

Most of us are not as generous as Mary, nor are we as grasping as Judas. Yet the same impulses that moved their hearts can move ours. On the one hand, there may be a bit of Judas in us. However pure our intentions once might have been, we may find ourselves taking more than we give, using any status we have for our own benefit, capitalizing on our following of Christ for our own advantage. If we do not curb our self-seeking, our discipleship may end up like that of Judas.

On the other hand, we may also have an impulse to give all to Jesus, to gather up everything we own and everything we are in one bundle and lay it at his feet. That is the impulse of God's grace in us. Mary of Bethany can be our model, a model of giving to Jesus with abandon, of giving ourselves totally to him.

Those You Have Given Me

"I pray for them. I am not praying for the world, but for those you have given me, for they are yours. All I have is yours, and all you have is mine. And glory has come to me through them. I will remain in the world no longer, but they are still in the world, and I am coming to you. Holy Father, protect them by the power of your name — the name you gave me — so that they may be one as we are one. While I was with them, I protected them and kept them safe by that name you have given me" (Jn 17:9-12 NIV).

The Gospel of John presents us with a long prayer of Jesus at the close of the Last Supper. Jesus prays for his disciples, his closest friends, who are sharing this most sacred meal with him. But in his prayer he does not refer to them as his disciples or friends, although they most certainly were (see Jn 15:15, for example). Jesus instead prays to his Father for "those you have given me."

Jesus puts the accent on the disciples being chosen by and belonging to the Father, rather than on their having been chosen by him and belonging to him. Jesus acknowledges that the disciples were the Father's gift to him, rather than his own achievement. He sees the disciples as belonging to him only in the sense that he shares all the Father has, and they first belonged to the Father.

Jesus claims nothing as his own but acknowledges that whatever he has came from his Father. "They were yours; you gave them to me" (Jn 17:6 NIV).

Luke gives us a glimpse of this same reality when he presents the selection of the twelve apostles: "One of those days Jesus went out to a mountainside to pray, and spent the night praying to God. When morning came, he called his disciples to him and chose twelve of them, whom he also designated apostles" (Lk 6:12-13 NIV).

Jesus did not merely pray for God's guidance in the important matter of choosing the twelve apostles. Rather he asked in prayer who his Father had chosen and was entrusting to him. The difference may be subtle, but it is important: It is the difference between asking someone for his advice in a certain matter and asking him what decision he has made in the matter.

Jesus' attitude toward his followers has an application in our lives. Although our relationship with the Father is different from that of Jesus, we participate in his sonship and can truly consider ourselves children of God. We can also consider those with whom we have a special relationship to be those whom God has given us: our spouse, our children, our parents, other members of our family, our friends, our co-workers.

These people are not a part of our lives because of any special revelation we have received from God; they are there because of choices we have made or because of circumstances, some of them accidental. But we can consider them to be those whom God has given us. In some way they are each in our care.

What is at issue is how we look at them. Do we consider the people in our lives to be satellites orbiting around us, existing at our pleasure and for our service? Or do we hold them as people who belong to God, as ones he has created and is redeeming, as those whom, in his providence, he has made a part of our lives and given us an opportunity to serve? Are they "my" family and friends, or are they children of God, loaned to my care?

The example of Jesus in his relationship with his disciples sets the pattern for us. He was concerned for his disciples' well-being, concerned to keep them true to their call from God. He taught them and, as is evident from John 17, he prayed for them.

Above all, Jesus loved those the Father had given him. He put up with their inconsistencies and failures; he did not draw back from loving them even when they betrayed him. He gave himself up for their sake, for they had been given to him by his Father. He would invite us to do the same for those whom the Father has given us.

Simon of Cyrene

They . . . led him out to crucify him. They pressed into service a passer-by, Simon, a Cyrenian, who was coming in from the country, the father of Alexander and Rufus, to carry his cross (Mk 15:20-21).

Power has its privileges, and one of the privileges that Roman soldiers enjoyed in the lands in which they were stationed was the right to press local civilians into service. A Roman soldier could select someone at random to come with him and carry his baggage. According to one writer, "the sign of impressment was a tap on the shoulder with the flat of a Roman spear."

Jesus had this practice in mind when he taught his followers, "Should anyone press you into service for one mile, go with him for two miles" (Mt 5:41). Jews resented being treated like pack animals by Roman soldiers, so Jesus' command probably shocked the disciples. Yet this teaching of Jesus is no more shocking than some of his other commands — to love our enemies, for example (see Mt 5:43-48).

One of those who was pressed into service at the whim of Roman soldiers was a certain Simon from Cyrene. Cyrene was a city on the north coast of Africa, in what is present-day Libya, with a sizable Jewish population. Simon had either moved from Cyrene to Jerusalem (perhaps owning land there), or had come to Jerusalem to celebrate the feast of Passover. In any case, he was passing by when Roman soldiers needed someone to carry Jesus' cross, and they picked Simon. There is no indication that their choice of him was anything other than arbitrary; there is no indication that Simon was a disciple of Jesus.

Yet when Simon took the cross of Jesus on his own shoulders and carried it behind Jesus (see Lk 23:26), he fulfilled what Jesus demanded of his disciples: "If anyone wishes to come after me, he must deny himself and take up his cross daily and follow me" (Lk 9:23); "Whoever does not carry his own cross and come after me cannot be my disciple" (Lk 14:27). Simon of Cyrene gives us a snapshot of discipleship: following after Jesus, carrying his cross.

What happened afterwards? Did Simon drop off the cross at Calvary, walk home, and forget the whole affair? There are good reasons to believe otherwise. Mark describes Simon as "the father of Alexander and Rufus," as if Alexander and Rufus were Christians known by his readers. According to ancient tradition, Mark's Gospel was written in Rome. Paul, in his letter to Rome, writes, "Greet Rufus, chosen in the Lord; and greet his mother — a mother to me also" (Rom 16:13 NRSV). It would seem that Simon's carrying of Jesus' cross was a turning point for him and his family.

But no matter what became of Simon afterwards, his deed that day earned him a place in the Gospels, and in our reflections on what it means to be a disciple of Jesus. All of us are familiar with the idea of "carrying our crosses" in life. We usually think of our crosses in terms of some sort of suffering that we cannot escape: perhaps a chronic illness, perhaps a difficult family situation, perhaps an irreparable harm done to us.

The example of Simon would throw a different light on what it means to follow after Jesus carrying a cross: It can mean shouldering the crosses of others, relieving them of their burdens and taking them on ourselves. That is what Simon did for Jesus, however involuntarily. And that is what Jesus asks us to do, voluntarily, going even the extra mile.

Paul wrote, "Bear one another's burdens, and so you will fulfill the law of Christ" (Gal 6:2). Take the sufferings of others upon yourself, just as Jesus bore the cross of our infirmities (see Is 53:4), just as Simon bore the cross of Jesus. Follow after Jesus, carrying not only your personal cross, whatever it may be, but also crosses of others that you have shouldered — for in doing so you, like Simon, bear the cross of Christ.

Forgotten Sisters

Standing by the cross of Jesus were his mother and his mother's sister, Mary the wife of Clopas, and Mary of Magdala (Jn 19:25).

Was Mary an only child? We usually don't think of Mary having any brothers or sisters. They are not mentioned in the ancient writings that claim to provide details about the life of Mary not recorded in the Gospels. There is devotion to Mary's parents, saints Joachim and Anne, but none, as far as I know, to any sister of Mary.

Yet there she is — Mary's sister — in John's Gospel, standing by the cross of Jesus along with Mary, and two other Marys.

Some speculate that the name of Mary's sister was Salome and that she was the wife of Zebedee and the mother of James and John, basing their speculation on a combination of Matthew 27:56 and Mark 15:40. This would make James and John cousins of Jesus, and might explain why they thought they were due places of honor in Jesus' kingdom (see Mk 10:35-37). But the evidence for such speculation is thin. The only certainty we have is that Mary did have a sister, and she was present at the crucifixion.

Trick question number two: Was Paul an only child?

Paul never mentions having any brothers or sisters in his letters, nor do any make an appearance in Acts. But there is again a single verse to upset our preconceptions: "The son of Paul's sister, however, heard about the ambush; so he went and entered the compound and reported it to Paul" (Acts 23:16). Paul had a sister who lived long enough to marry and bear a son. Perhaps she even outlived Paul: We have no way of knowing. We do not even know her name.

It would be nice to know more about these two forgotten

sisters. What stories they could tell! Was Mary's sister present at the wedding feast at Cana? What was her reaction to the events of that day? What did Paul's sister think of her feisty brother? Was he a pain in the neck when they were growing up?

We will never know — at least in this life. Scripture provides us with no access to the thoughts of these two women, and Scripture is the only reliable source of information we have about them.

Do these two largely overlooked sisters have any lessons for us?

These sisters are reminders of the nature of Scripture. The Bible was not written to provide us with complete biographies of Jesus and of our ancestors in the faith. The purpose of Scripture is to teach "firmly, faithfully, and without error that truth which God wanted put into the sacred writings for the sake of our salvation" (Vatican II, *Dei Verbum*, no. 11). In providing us with saving truth, Scripture gives us glimpses of the lives of many people — above all Jesus. But the Bible does not aim at biographical completeness: It doesn't fill in all the blanks we might like to see filled in. These sisters are two of the blanks.

These two women also bear a second message for us. Most Christians through the ages — most of those with whom we will share heaven — are anonymous. Most lived ordinary lives and were soon forgotten by all except their immediate descendants. Most of us will follow in their quickly forgotten footsteps.

These two virtually forgotten sisters can serve as patron saints for all of the forgotten Christians through the ages, and for us as well. We don't have to be famous to go to heaven, or have extraordinary accomplishments that get written up in history books. We need to find salvation through Jesus, but that is all we need. Even if we are as quickly forgotten, as were the sisters of Mary and Paul, we can still obtain the greatest prize that any human being can ever achieve: eternal life with God.

And once we are in heaven, these will be two interesting women to chat with!

Remember Me

When they came to the place called the Skull, they crucified him and the criminals there, one on his right, the other on his left.

Now one of the criminals hanging there reviled Jesus, saying, "Are you not the Messiah? Save yourself and us." The other, however, rebuking him, said in reply, "Have you no fear of God, for you are subject to the same condemnation? And indeed, we have been condemned justly, for the sentence we received corresponds to our crimes, but this man has done nothing criminal." Then he said, "Jesus, remember me when you come into your kingdom." He replied to him, "Amen, I say to you, today you will be with me in Paradise" (Lk 23:33, 39-43).

Crucifixion was death by public torture, a slow and horrible form of execution. It was a sentence usually reserved for violent criminals and insurrectionists. We are not told what the two men executed with Jesus had done to deserve crucifixion, but, by the admission of one of them, it was serious enough to merit this agonizing death.

We should therefore not romanticize the "good thief," imagining him to be a noble person who happened to steal for a living — a "robber with a heart of gold." It is better to take him at his word: He had committed crimes deserving of the worst punishment.

Yet even this criminal could recognize that Jesus' death

was a set-up. The inscription over Jesus' head read, "This is the King of the Jews" (Lk 23:38). If this is interpreted as the legal charge against Jesus, then Jesus was being executed for inciting rebellion against Roman rule — a patently false charge (see Lk 23:2-5,14-15).

The inscription was put up to mock Jesus. It was one more taunt in crescendo of mockery on Calvary that day. "If you are King of the Jews, save yourself" (Lk 23:37) was the jeer of the religious leaders and Roman soldiers and even one of the criminals being executed with Jesus. It was like — but far worse than — a drunken crowd on a boat throwing someone overboard and saying, "If you can swim, now prove it," and laughing as the person drowned.

One of the criminals refused to join in this mockery. Even though he had committed serious crimes, he still could tell the difference between deserved and undeserved punishment. Jesus did not deserve to be crucified and jeered at, and this criminal said so.

He also said, "Jesus, remember me when you come into your kingdom" (Lk 23:42). He did not address Jesus with the title "Lord," as a follower of Jesus might have done, so we should be wary of reading too full an act of faith into his words. He simply called to Jesus by name, and asked to be remembered when Jesus came into his kingdom.

How much did this criminal know or understand of Jesus' kingdom? Unless he was given some direct revelation by God it was probably not much: Even those who had followed Jesus throughout his public ministry still did not really understand the nature of his kingdom (see Acts 1:6).

In essence, what this criminal did was "unmock" Jesus. He acknowledged the truth that everyone else was conspiring to obscure with their jeers: Jesus was being unjustly put to death. He took the taunts being heaped on Jesus and turned them into a respectful request. Where others mocked Jesus by calling him a Messiah-king, this criminal spoke to him as if he really were a king, and would have power to dispense favors.

"Remember me, criminal though I am, when you begin your reign." Jesus in response said that he would indeed remember him, and that they would be together that day in Paradise. This man who deserved the wretched death of crucifixion became, in a sense, the first canonized saint, the only saint canonized by Jesus himself. What a glorious reward for a few respectful words — uttered by one who had committed serious sins and may not have understood all that much about Jesus.

The cross is an index of God's love for us, an index of the lengths to which he will go to forgive us. Jesus' canonization of a criminal who died beside him is an indication of what he wants to do for everyone. We can certainly make at least as much response to Jesus as did this criminal — and hope for as great a reward.

The First Witness

But Mary stayed outside the tomb weeping.
Jesus said to her, "Mary!" She turned and said
to him in Hebrew, "Rabbouni," which means
Teacher. Jesus said to her, "Stop holding on to me,
for I have not yet ascended to the Father. But go to
my brothers and tell them, 'I am going to my Father
and your Father, to my God and your God.' " Mary
of Magdala went and announced to the disciples, "I
have seen the Lord," and what he told her (Jn 20:11,
16-18).

Mary Magdalene is often thought of as something she was not, and too infrequently remembered for what she was.

The Bible nowhere describes Mary Magdalene as a prostitute. It does say that she was one of the women "who had been cured of evil spirits and infirmities," and that "seven demons had gone out" of her (see Lk 8:2).

Could these seven demons have manifested themselves in sexual immorality? Jesus' casting out of demons is often linked with physical healings (see Lk 4:40-41; 6:17-19), including the healing of such afflictions as muteness (see Mt 9:32-33) and curvature of the spine (see Lk 13:11-13). In other cases demon possession caused mental disorders or convulsions (see Mk 5:2-5; 9:17-29). But the Gospels describe no instance of Jesus expelling a demon of prostitution.

Therefore, if Mary Magdalene was one of those whom Jesus had "cured of evil spirits and infirmities" (Lk 8:2), the plausible interpretation is that she had been healed of some physical affliction by Jesus, even multiple afflictions.

How then did she enter into popular lore as a prostitute? In about the sixth century, she became identified with the un-named "sinful woman" who anointed Jesus' feet (see Lk 7:36-50). But Luke does not make this identification; he intro-duces Mary Magdalene a few verses later as if for the first time (see Lk 8:2), implying that they were different women.

Even if Mary Magdalene was this "sinful woman," what basis is there for concluding that her sin was prostitution? Are women capable of no other sin? What does it say about one's view of women if one imagines that a woman's sins must be sexual in nature?

If Scripture does not portray Mary Magdalene as a prosti-tute, how does it portray her? She followed Jesus as he traveled about in Galilee; she was one of the women who took care of Jesus and of other disciples out of their own resources (see Lk 8:1-3). She followed him all the way to Jerusalem, and she did not run away in his hour of crisis. She was a witness to the crucifixion of Jesus (see Mk 15:40-41; Jn 19:25), and a wit-ness to his burial as well.

Most importantly, Mary Magdalene was a witness to the resurrection of Jesus. She arose early Easter morning to go to the tomb of Jesus to anoint his body. Some disciples hid behind locked doors out of fear (see Jn 20:19), but Mary Magdalene and a few other women bravely ventured forth, going out a gate of Jerusalem and past the hump of Calvary on their way to the tomb of Jesus (see Mk 16:1-2; Jn 20:1). The tomb was empty, and an angel told the women that Jesus was risen from the dead. In John's account, Mary remains at the tomb and the risen Jesus appears to her — the first to whom he manifests himself (see Jn 20:11-18). The longer ending of Mark's Gospel preserves the same tradition: "When he had risen, early on the first day of the week, he appeared first to Mary Magdalene" (Mk 16:9). Mary Magdalene is commissioned to tell the other disciples about the risen Lord (see Jn 20:17).

How then does Scripture present Mary Magdalene to us? As one who had been healed by Jesus, and who quietly served him during his public ministry. As one who followed him to the end, even after others ran away. As one who continued to serve Jesus even in his death, and consequently became the first to see her risen Lord. Mary Magdalene deserves a special place of honor among the followers of Jesus, as one who served him faithfully and was the first witness to his resurrection.

4

Walking With Jesus
Day by Day

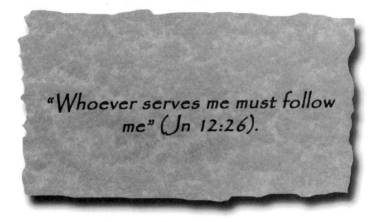

"*Whoever serves me must follow me*" (Jn 12:26).

Ordinary Time

After this, Jesus revealed himself again to his disciples at the Sea of Tiberias. He revealed himself in this way. Together were Simon Peter, Thomas called Didymus, Nathanael from Cana in Galilee, Zebedee's sons, and two others of his disciples. Simon Peter said to them, "I am going fishing." They said to him, "We also will come with you." So they went out and got into the boat, but that night they caught nothing. When it was already dawn, Jesus was standing on the shore; but the disciples did not realize that it was Jesus.

When they climbed out on shore, they saw a charcoal fire with fish on it and bread.

Jesus said to them, "Come, have breakfast" (Jn 21:1-4, 9, 12 JB).

The greater part of the Catholic Church's liturgical year has traditionally been called "ordinary time." There are special seasons within the liturgical year — the seasons of Advent, Christmas, Lent, and Easter — but the time between these special seasons is simply "ordinary time." This time might be considered merely the leftovers from more important seasons, but in fact it makes up most of the liturgical year — over thirty Sundays.

Advent is a time of looking forward to the coming of Jesus Christ; the Christmas season celebrates his coming. Lent is a special time of repentance; the Easter season celebrates Christ's resurrection, ascension, and sending of the Holy Spirit. But what do we do or celebrate during the remaining part of the year? Is it simply an empty lull while we await the beginning of the next series of important feasts?

I think the fact that most of the Church's year is simply "ordinary time" has a message for us. Most of our lives are taken up with quite ordinary living. There are moments when we experience God's grace in a special way; there are key turning points in our lives. But there are broad valleys between our mountaintop experiences. Even if our memories and hopes are focused on the mountaintops, most of our lives are lived in the valleys.

Jesus spent approximately thirty years living an apparently quiet life in Nazareth before he began his public ministry. He presumably spent most of his time doing the same things that fill our hours: working to earn a living, eating, sleeping, talking with his neighbors.

Jesus also spent much time reading the Scriptures and praying. But to his neighbors he appeared to be a fairly normal person, for they were later astonished when he began teaching: "Where did the man get all this? This is the carpenter, surely, the son of Mary" (Mk 6:2, 3 JB). Although the Gospels highlight the public ministry of Jesus, most of his life was spent in "ordinary time."

There is also an ordinariness about Peter's and six other disciples' going fishing after the resurrection. We find them back on the Sea of Galilee, where they were first called. They were commercial fishermen, not sport fishermen, and they were again at their work.

Jesus appears to these disciples, but his appearance is somehow so ordinary that they do not recognize him at first. He gives them a great catch of fish but he also fixes breakfast for them, knowing that they must be hungry after a long night of work. How ordinary!

The special seasons of the Church's year and the special moments of grace in our lives are important. But so are the ordinary times. In the long run it is how faithful we are to Christ day-in and day-out that determines how closely we follow him. The fruits of the Spirit — love, joy, peace, patience, kindness, and the rest — should be the earmarks of how we live every day, not just special moments of grace now and then.

In the Holy Land there are many mountains and valleys. The mountaintops give a breathtaking view of the surrounding countryside, but good cropland is found only in the valleys. And the broader the valley, the greater the expanse of crops that can be grown.

There is a reason why most of our lives are lived in the valleys, in "ordinary time": It is in the valleys that our lives are to bear fruit for the Lord.

Prodigal II

"Now the older son had been out in the field and, on his way back, as he neared the house, he heard the sound of music and dancing.

"He became angry, and when he refused to enter the house, his father came out and pleaded with him. He said to his father in reply, 'Look, all these years I served you and not once did I disobey your orders; yet you never gave me even a young goat to feast on with my friends.'

He said to him, 'My son, you are here with me always; everything I have is yours' " (Lk 15:25, 28-29, 31).

The younger brother in Jesus' parable was certainly a prodigal son: He "squandered his inheritance on a life of dissipation" (Lk 15:13). He squandered not only his father's money but also his father's love: He had demanded his inheritance while his father was still alive, which in effect said to his father, "I can't wait for you to die."

But the older brother was also a prodigal son. While he did not squander his father's money, he did squander his love. And while his younger brother recognized that he had sinned against heaven and against his father (see Lk 15:21), the parable ends with the older brother still blind to his prodigality.

His father told him, "You are here with me always; everything I have is yours." These statements could be interpreted in a legal sense: The older brother's place of residence was the family farm, and as the sole remaining heir, the entire farm was his heritage. But the father wasn't talking about legal matters; he was talking about his relationship with his son. "You are with me always; all I have is yours" are words one speaks to a beloved quite apart from matters of property deeds and legal residence.

The older son, however, thought of his relationship with his father in terms of working for him and not disobeying him. "All these years I served you" could more literally be translated, "All these years I slaved for you" or "All these years I have been serving you like a slave." With employees, normal considerations are productivity, length of service, and obeying work rules. Those were the standards by which the older son judged himself. For all practical purposes, he thought of his father as his employer.

The older son likewise treated the farm not as his heritage, but as his father's possession. He resented his father for not giving him a goat for a party, while his father's attitude would have been, "Of course, have a goat! Have a dozen goats! They are all yours!"

The older son distanced himself from his father, as is hinted by the spatial imagery of the parable. He was "out in the field," and "refused to enter the house." He did not go to his father; his father came to him. The parable ends with him still outside, and his father pleading for him to enter.

Can we see something of ourselves in this older prodigal son? We may be good at not breaking God's commandments, although probably not to the point of being able to claim, "Not once did I disobey your orders." But God would like more from us than avoidance of sin.

Again, we may be diligent in serving God, carrying out apostolic activities and performing works of mercy. Others may surely benefit from our efforts, but God wants more from us than our service: God wants *us*. Jesus told his followers "I no longer call you slaves [or servants], because a slave does not know what his master is doing. I have called you friends" (Jn 15:15).

God wants to enter into personal relationship with us. That is why he revealed himself to us through his Son, Jesus. That is why he calls us to be with him for eternity: not to keep us out of sin, not so that we can sweep up the floors of heaven, but so that we can see him face-to-face. If we are willing to settle for anything less, we too are being prodigal with a Father's love for us.

Open Our Eyes

As he passed by he saw a man blind from birth. . . . He spat on the ground and made clay with the saliva, and smeared the clay on his eyes, and said to him, "Go wash in the Pool of Siloam" (which means Sent). So he went and washed, and came back able to see. So they said to him, "[So] how were your eyes opened?" He replied, "The man called Jesus made clay and anointed my eyes and told me, 'Go to Siloam and wash.' So I went there and washed and was able to see." And they said to him, "Where is he?" He said, "I don't know." When Jesus heard that they had thrown him out, he found him and said, "Do you believe in the Son of Man?" He answered and said, "Who is he, sir, that I may believe in him?" Jesus said to him, "You have seen him and the one speaking with you is he." He said, "I do believe, Lord," and he worshiped him (Jn 9:1, 6-7, 10-12, 35-38).

John's account of Jesus' opening the eyes of the man born blind takes up all of chapter nine of his Gospel, and carries a profound message about spiritual sight and blindness. Jesus proclaimed, "I am the light of the world" (Jn 9:5). He gave sight to the man born blind, and this man came to faith in him. On the other hand, the Pharisees could see but were blind to Jesus, and refused to believe in him.

There are lessons for both in the blind man receiving sight, and in the Pharisees being blind with seeing eyes.

The man born blind had to have his eyes opened by Jesus
to be able to see him. Even then, he really didn't know who
Jesus was or where he could be found. Jesus had to not only
heal the eyes of this man, but explain to him what he saw. "You
have seen the Son of Man," Jesus said to him; "You are looking at him and speaking with him now."

The blind man only gradually realized who Jesus was —
which is to say, the blind man progressively grew in faith. At
first he thought that "the man called Jesus" healed him (Jn
9:11). Then he realized that this man who had the power to
heal must have been sent by God, and therefore said, "He is a
prophet" (9:17). Finally he came to full faith and called Jesus
"Lord," a title applied to God himself: "He said, 'I do believe,
Lord,' and he worshiped him" (9:38).

Our own life of faith is also a matter of growth, of gradually realizing ever more fully who Jesus is. It is Jesus who
draws us along this path, just as Jesus took the initiative to heal
this blind man — who did not ask to be healed — and then
later sought him out again (see Jn 9:35). We need to respond at
each step of the way. But our own condition is always one of
relative blindness. Jesus must heal us of the condition that prevents us from fully seeing and accepting him.

The Pharisees, on the other hand, remained blind from start
to finish. There was no growth in their understanding of Jesus.
They saw him with human eyes, but saw him only as human.
Jesus could not heal their blindness because they refused to
admit that they were blind. He told them, "If you were blind,
you would have no sin; but now you are saying, 'We see,' so
your sin remains" (Jn 9:41).

Just as the blind man stands for all of us, so do the Pharisees. They were people who thought themselves religious and
in compliance with God's commands. It was largely because
they thought they were already pleasing to God that they were
blind to what God wanted to do for them through Jesus. Their
religiosity was a shield against grace; their being sure they
knew who Jesus was (see Jn 9:24) prevented them from really

realizing who Jesus was. Their thinking they saw was their blindness — the worst form of blindness.

Once we have been touched and healed by Jesus, it is easy to fall into the Pharisee's mistake. But one message from chapter nine of John's Gospel is that we are always relatively blind, and always only relatively healed. Faith is a matter of growth, not a once-and-for-all achievement. It is far better for us to cry out to Jesus to heal our blindness than think we have 20/20 spiritual sight.

The Rebukes of Jesus

Jesus turned and rebuked them (Lk 9:55).

What does Jesus expect of us as his disciples?

The Gospels certainly give us a wealth of his teachings and expectations, from the Sermon on the Mount (see Mt 5-7) to his Last Supper discourse (see Jn 13-16). Meditating on these teachings and molding ourselves in accordance with them is the work of a lifetime.

Yet the Gospels also give us some more specific clues of what Jesus expects of us, in that they describe Jesus rebuking or correcting his disciples on a number of occasions. Certainly anything Jesus had to rebuke in his first followers is something he would find equally abhorrent in us. By meditating on the rebukes of Jesus to his disciples we can therefore get a clearer understanding of his expectations of us.

One series of rebukes or corrections had to do with the disciples' lack of faith and trust in Jesus. Jesus was disappointed that they became afraid during a storm at sea, even though he was in the boat with them (see Mt 8:23-26). He chastised Peter for having such little faith after he had invited him to step out of the boat (see Mt 14:22-33). He rebuked his disciples for being faithless when they could not cure a possessed boy (see Mt 17:14-20). Even after his resurrection he had to chastise the disciples for being fearful and doubting (see Lk 24:36-40; Jn 20:27). Jesus expects his followers to have faith-filled trust in him.

Another series of Jesus' corrections had to do with the disciples' lack of understanding. He was disappointed that they did not understand his parables (see Mk 4:13) and sometimes seemed to have no more comprehension of his teachings than the crowds (see Mk 7:18). He seemed exasperated when they missed the point of his words (see Mk 8:14-21).

Their lack of understanding was particularly serious when it had to do with the nature of Jesus' mission and the nature of the kingdom he came to establish, and these misunderstandings earned Jesus' sternest rebukes. When Jesus taught that he would offer up his life as the Messiah and Peter rejected this, Jesus "rebuked Peter and said, 'Get behind me, Satan. You are thinking not as God does, but as human beings do' " (Mk 8:33). When the disciples, likewise thinking that they were to be part of a kingdom of triumphant power, wanted to call down fire on an inhospitable Samaritan town, Jesus again rebuked them (see Lk 9:51-56). And at the end, when they tried to prevent Jesus' arrest with the sword, Jesus had to correct them (see Mt 26:51-54).

Because the disciples had their minds set on a kingdom of this world, they consequently were concerned about who should have the most honor and power within it. Their jockeying for position earned Jesus' repeated correction. He taught them that anyone who wanted to be first must be the servant of all, just as he had come to serve and give his life as a ransom for many (see Mk 9:30-37; 10:35-45). Luke presents us with the sorry picture of Jesus' having to break up a dispute among them over who was greatest that was interrupting the Last Supper (see Lk 22:24-27)!

The disciples earned the rebuke of Jesus on other occasions as well: He was indignant when they tried to prevent children from coming to him (see Mk 10:13-16); he prevented his disciples from obstructing a man who was casting out demons in his name (see Mk 9:38-40); he defended a woman who anointed him against the disciples' criticisms (see Mk 14:3-9); he chastised his three closest friends for not keeping watch with him in the Garden of Gethsemane on the night before he died (see Mk 14:32-42).

All of these rebukes and corrections of Jesus should give us pause. Are we disappointing him, as his first followers did? Are we reluctant to put our full faith and trust in him? Are we slow to understand and accept his teaching? Do we secretly wish that his kingdom was one of honor and power instead of service and self-sacrifice? Are we looking out for ourselves even as we walk alongside him? Do we dispute with each other as if he were not present?

Such self-examination may prove sobering. Yet we should also keep in mind that Jesus never cut off his disciples from himself, even if he had to rebuke them. He corrected them only so that they could walk more closely with him on his way to the Father.

Pilgrim Farmers

"I tell you, open your eyes and look at the fields! They are ripe for harvest. Even now the reaper draws his wages, even now he harvests the crop for eternal life, so that the sower and the reaper may be glad together. Thus the saying 'One sows and another reaps' is true. I sent you to reap what you have not worked for. Others have done the hard work, and you have reaped the benefits of their labor" (Jn 4:35-38 NIV).

Jesus often drew examples and comparisons from farming in his teaching because many of his listeners were farmers. Even those who did not farm for a living were intimately acquainted with farming. For example, those who fished the Sea of Galilee beached their boats only a few yards from cultivated fields. No one was ignorant of what it meant to sow and to reap.

No one was ignorant of the meaning of the proverb "One sows, another reaps." It was a pessimistic saying reflecting the uneven fortunes of life. A man could sow and be killed in battle before harvest or otherwise not live long enough to enjoy the fruit of his harvest (see Dt 20:6; Lk 12:16-20).

But Jesus gave this proverb a different and more positive meaning: We, as his followers, reap what others have sown. In the immediate context of John's Gospel, Jesus is referring to the harvest of converts that his apostles shall reap. St. Paul uses a very similar analogy when he writes, "I planted the seed, Apollos watered it, but God made it grow" (1 Cor 3:6 NIV). The harvest of the kingdom is the result of many working together as servants of God, each carrying out his or her part and benefiting from the work of others.

These words of Jesus also carry a broader meaning. Our Christian life is enriched by all those who have preceded us on the journey to our Father. We reap the benefits of their theological reflection on the mysteries of God; we reap the harvest of their evangelism; we enjoy the fruit of their labors and sacrifice. Our Christian life is a gift given to us by God, working through others as his intermediaries. There is nothing we possess that we have not been given: "What do you have that you have not received?" (1 Cor 4:7 NIV).

This truth should teach us humility and gratitude. We are reaping what others have sown; we are the beneficiaries of their hard labor.

This truth should also help us keep our own labors in proper perspective. We too do our share of sowing what others will reap. We will not be on this earth long enough to reap all that we have sown — either for good or for bad. If we have been the cause of scandal and loss of faith in others, we will only find out the full extent of our sin at the Last Judgment, when Jesus confronts us with the harvest that our actions have yielded. And if we have been the occasion of faith and growth in others we likewise will not fully realize the good fruit of our efforts until that final day. If not even a cup of cold water given or withheld is to be forgotten on that day (see Mt 25:31-46), assuredly all that we have done or failed to do for Jesus will be remembered.

While farming provides a good analogy for some important aspects of the Christian life, it is an analogy with limitations. Farmers must stay in one place, at least long enough to attempt to harvest the crop they have planted. Discipleship, on the other hand, is fittingly symbolized as a journey: It is our following after Christ, our walking in his footsteps. In our journey with him who had no place to lay his head, we are constantly on the move.

Perhaps there is a way of combining these two images, the

image of farming and the image of being on a journey. We might think of ourselves as pilgrim or migratory farmers: men and women who follow after Jesus, reaping the harvests he leads us to and at the same time sowing crops for those who will come after us. What we have, we have received from those who have gone before us, sowing as they went. All that we do will result in a harvest for those who come after us — a good harvest if we sow well, a thin harvest if we do not.

Pilgrim farmers never know how the crops they have sown turn out, for they must move on to other fields before harvest time. They must take it on faith that their service of Jesus will result in good harvests for others, until that day when sower and reaper rejoice together in the eternal presence of God and enjoy the final fruit of their actions.

Jesus Walks Ahead

They were on their way up to Jerusalem, with Jesus leading the way, and the disciples were astonished, while those who followed were afraid. Again he took the Twelve aside and told them what was going to happen to him. "We are going up to Jerusalem," he said, "and the Son of Man will be betrayed to the chief priests and teachers of the law. They will condemn him to death and will hand him over to the Gentiles, who will mock him and spit on him, flog him and kill him. Three days later he will rise" (Mk 10:32-34 NIV).

Mark's Gospel conveys its message through images as well as words. Here we have the image of Jesus walking on ahead of his apostles. It is an image of discipleship: To be a disciple means to follow in the footsteps of Jesus.

But this passage from Mark conveys a very sobering image of discipleship. Those who follow after Jesus are described as being dazed and fearful. Jesus has been telling them about his coming death (see Mk 8:31; 9:31), but they cannot understand what he is talking about (see Mk 9:32). Peter has even tried to tell Jesus that he shouldn't make such gloomy predictions (see Mk 8:32).

But Jesus insisted on what he was saying: He was on his way to Jerusalem to die, and to die a particularly unpleasant death. No wonder his followers walked behind him on the road in apprehension and fear. They had no desire to watch their Lord being spat on and mocked and tortured, even if he did promise that he would overcome death.

There was probably another factor as well to their fear. In the passages immediately preceding and following Mark's description of Jesus walking ahead on the road to Jerusalem, the apostles express concern about themselves. Peter asks what they will receive, since they have given up everything to follow Jesus (see Mk 10:28 and Mt 19:27). Then James and John ask for favored places when Jesus comes into his glory (see Mk 10:35-36).

The apostles were not only fearful for what might happen to Jesus; they were also fearful about what would happen to them if Jesus met the fate that he said awaited him. And indeed, Jesus had made it clear that the path of the master had to be the path of the disciples "If anyone would come after me, he must deny himself and take up his cross and follow me" (Mk 8:34 NIV).

No wonder the disciples lagged behind Jesus on the road to Jerusalem: They did not like where he was leading them. And yet, despite their fears, he was leading them to resurrection. The path he was taking was the best possible path for them to walk. Even if they were filled with dread and uncertainty, they would shortly experience his triumph over death and participate in it themselves.

Jesus likewise walks ahead of us. He is the "pioneer" (Heb 12:2 NRSV) who has blazed the path that we follow in faith.

But alas, sometimes he seems to walk too far ahead of us. We would prefer his being constantly at our side, giving us his arm to help us over obstacles on the road. We would prefer that he make more frequent rest stops, to give us a chance to catch our breath.

Above all, we would prefer that he not take us along a path that leads to suffering or trials. When he allowed us to sit with him by the shore of a tranquil lake and listen to him speak to us, then our hearts burned within us at his words. Now that he walks ahead of us to Calvary we are fearful and apprehensive.

But the important fact is that he does walk ahead of us. Our only hope for remaining in union with him is to follow after him, wherever he leads us. We cannot remain sitting by the side of the lake after he has set out for Jerusalem, or we will lose sight of him.

On the other hand, if we do follow after him despite our uncertainty and apprehension, then where he is we shall also be (see Jn 14:3). That is our comfort, our hope, our source of strength: No matter how dark the path of discipleship, Jesus walks ahead of us and will be awaiting us at its end. He asks us to go nowhere that he has not already gone. He asks us to endure nothing that will not result in resurrection. The path that he has blazed for us leads to life. He walks ahead of us and leads us along, as he led his first followers to Jerusalem.

Daily Cross, Daily Bread

Then he said to all, "If anyone wishes to come after me, he must deny himself and take up his cross daily and follow me" (Lk 9:23).
He said to them, "When you pray, say:
Father, hallowed be your name,
your kingdom come.
Give us each day our daily bread" (Lk 11:2-3).

In Luke's Gospel, Jesus twice uses the word "daily" in special instructions to his disciples. We must take up our crosses daily if we are to follow him. We are to pray that our Father will give us each day our daily bread. Is there any connection between these two daily dimensions of discipleship?

Let us look first at the crosses Jesus asks us to bear. All of us have our own particular crosses, but some of them are shaped alike. Chronic sickness or infirmity, financial hardships, the struggle to overcome addictions or depression — the list goes on and includes whatever burdens make our shoulders ache with fatigue.

We cannot rid ourselves of these crosses with a snap of our fingers, and so we must follow Jesus, bearing their weight. This means not losing faith, not giving up hope, not letting our charity grow cold, despite the burdens we bear. Even if we fall beneath the weight of these crosses, we must get up again and stagger after Jesus.

In light of these crosses, what does it mean to pray for daily bread? Since bread was the staple food in the biblical world, bread symbolized all food, all sustenance. To pray for daily bread meant more than praying for two slices of Wonder Bread for our luncheon sandwich. "Give us each day our daily bread" means "give us each day all that we need to sustain us for that day."

One of our daily needs is the particular strength to bear our particular crosses. For those infirm, it is the strength to bear the pain and debility of the infirmity that day. For an alcoholic, it is the grace not to drink that day. For whatever weighs us down, it is the strength to follow Jesus with that burden, trusting in him, clinging to him that day. That is the daily bread we ask from our Father.

While many crosses are involuntary, there are also crosses that we can choose to shoulder or not. A good deal of Christian service falls into this category. We can turn away from the needs of others, or we can try to help meet their needs . . . usually at some cost to us. We can use the gifts that God has given us as he would have us use them, or we can pretend that we are ungifted. We can take the crosses of others on our shoulders, or we can stand idly by, merely feeling sorry that they suffer.

"Give us each day our daily bread" can also therefore be a prayer for the strength and love to bear the crosses of others, to shift some of the weight from their shoulders to ours. It can be a prayer for the grace to persevere in using our gifts of service, no matter how bored or fatigued we may have become. It can be a prayer that God will sustain us that day as care givers and comforters who, like Simon of Cyrene, follow after Jesus bearing another's cross.

"Give us each day our daily bread" can even mean, "Give me today a cross to bear." Why would we ever want to pray for a cross? Simply because Jesus does not invite us to follow him empty-shouldered. If our shoulders are free, there are plenty of crosses in this world, more than enough to go around. Jesus went to his Father bearing a cross, and he asks those who would follow him to do the same. Paul wrote, "Bear one another's burdens, and so you will fulfill the law of Christ" (Gal 6:2). And so we can pray, Give us each day the bread of bearing another's burdens.

Following Jesus

When the days for his being taken up were fulfilled, he resolutely determined to journey to Jerusalem (Lk 9:51).

Most of us dislike change — especially changes that are forced upon us. Our jobs might not be perfect, but it is very unsettling when our company goes out of business and we have to find new work. Moving to another city is a difficult disruption for many families. The death of a spouse or parent or child is a heavy blow, and our loved one's absence leaves a lingering emptiness. The list of painful changes goes on and on: loss of health, the limitations inherent in aging, old forms of prayer no longer seeming to work, upheaval in our parish.

Luke constructed his Gospel with a major pivot point of change. Verse 51 of chapter 9 marks the beginning of Jesus' journey to Jerusalem. Until this point, Jesus' ministry had been centered in Galilee. All of his followers were apparently Galileans (see Lk 22:59; 23:55; Acts 1:11). No mention is made in Luke's Gospel of Jesus having been back to Jerusalem after he was twelve years old.

Luke therefore portrays the journey to Jerusalem as a turning point in Jesus' public ministry, and devotes a considerable part of his Gospel to this journey. It is not only a change in geography but a change in the shape of Jesus' ministry. Put bluntly, Jesus went to Jerusalem to die: "When the days for his being taken up were fulfilled, he resolutely determined to journey to Jerusalem" (Lk 9:51).

Just before setting out on the journey to Jerusalem, Jesus told his followers what lay ahead: "The Son of Man must suffer greatly and be rejected . . . and be killed, and on the third day be raised" (Lk 9:22). Jesus had no suicidal tendencies, but he knew the inevitable outcome of remaining faithful to his Father's will for him. His followers, on the other hand, were slow to understand, even when be repeatedly told them where the journey would end: "But they did not understand this saying; its meaning was hidden from them so that they should not understand it, and they were afraid to ask him" (Lk 9:45).

We who have trouble accepting change can empathize with these first disciples. What trauma could be greater than having the one they followed as the Messiah face execution? What greater change could there be than from the Mount of Transfiguration (see Lk 9:28-36) to the Hill of Calvary? And what greater demand could face them than Jesus' invitation to follow in his footsteps and lose their lives for his sake? (see Lk 9:23-24).

It is no wonder then that they reacted to Jesus' words with fear and confusion, and followed in a daze: "They were on the way, going up to Jerusalem, and Jesus went ahead of them. They were amazed, and those who followed were afraid" (Mk 10:32).

What might this journey of Jesus and his disciples to Jerusalem mean to us as his followers today? I believe it is a warning that we cannot count on remaining forever in the familiar Galilean villages of our lives, and certainly not on the Mount of Transfiguration. There may come a point when the Jesus we follow sets out for Jerusalem, and to be with him we must go with him. We may have to kneel beside him in Gethsemane and join with him in praying, "Not my will but yours be done" (Lk 22:42).

I also believe that Luke's account of the journey of Jesus to Jerusalem provides us with instruction along the way (see Lk 9:51-21:37). Not everything that Luke includes in this section of his Gospel will apply to every one of us in all the changes we face, but if we read Luke's words as addressed to those who are in a time of transition, then I suspect we will find much in them that cuts through our confusion and instructs us, much that addresses our fears and assures us that we are still on the right path.

The Seed of Life

Jesus answered them, "The hour has come for the Son of Man to be glorified. Amen, amen, I say to you, unless a grain of wheat falls to the ground and dies, it remains just a grain of wheat; but if it dies, it produces much fruit. Whoever loves his life loses it, and whoever hates his life in this world will preserve it for eternal life. Whoever serves me must follow me, and where I am, there also will my servant be. The Father will honor whoever serves me" (Jn 12:23-26).

At Easter we celebrate the greatest mystery of our faith, the paschal mystery. It is a mystery of life through death: First of all, the death and resurrection of Jesus Christ, and secondly, our participation in his conquest of death.

To our normal human way of thinking, death is the ultimate evil, the ultimate tragedy, the ultimate negation. Yet Jesus calls his coming death his hour of glorification! This is a jolting reversal of human logic — akin to calling a severe famine a blessing, or leprosy an honor. To be executed on a cross is glorification? How can this possibly be?

Jesus uses an analogy to help us accept the logic of the cross. When a seed is planted, it is as if it has died and been buried. But a plant springs forth from this "dying," and when the seed is no more, the plant has taken its place. The plant is not the seed, but new life that has sprung forth from the seed. Should a seed refuse to be sown in the ground, it would remain a seed and eventually rot or dry up and lose its life. It is only in accepting the death of being sown that a seed is able to produce new and transformed life.

Jesus' eye was on the transformed life that he would have through dying, and therefore he could rightly call his dying his glorification. Jesus invites us to have the same faith and to follow him along the same path of life through death. To be a disciple of Jesus is ultimately a matter of letting him take us by the hand and lead us along the way of the cross, for that is the path to eternal life.

It is not an easy path, for it is a path of faith rather than sight. The seed that has been sown is no longer around to see the plant that springs forth. So too in this life we can see no farther than the loss of life in death, and not the new life that Jesus promises us. Our eyes can only see as far as our being sown in death; they cannot see the last stage of our journey with Jesus, when we are joined with him, transformed in the presence of his Father. We must follow after Jesus in faith.

Such faith is not always easy to sustain. Some of St. Paul's converts in Corinth doubted whether they would rise from the dead — a doubt that threatened the core of the Gospel message. Paul addresses this doubt in the fifteenth chapter of his first letter to Corinth: "If there is no resurrection of the dead, then neither has Christ been raised. And if Christ has not been raised, then empty [too] is our preaching; empty, too, your faith. If for this life only we have hoped in Christ, we are the most pitiable people of all" (1 Cor 15:13-14,19).

Paul makes use of the same seed-and-plant analogy as did Jesus in order to help his Corinthian converts embrace the mystery of life through death. "What you sow is not brought to life unless it dies. And what you sow is not the body that is to be but a bare kernel of wheat, perhaps, or of some other kind [of seed]; but God gives it a body as he chooses, and to each of the seeds its own body. So also is the resurrection of the dead. It is sown corruptible; it is raised incorruptible" (1 Cor 15:36-38, 42).

Our faith that we will follow Jesus through death to glorification should shape how we live this life. We do not need to waste our energies in a futile attempt to cling to this life and

the things of this life as if they are all we have. We are free to
devote ourselves totally to serving and following Jesus. We are
free to live in the present, because we do not need to be anxious about the eternal future. We can follow after Jesus even
along the way of the cross, because we know where the path
ends.

5

Teach Us to Pray

"Ask and you will receive; seek and you will find; knock and the door will be opened to you" (Lk 11:9).

Jesus' Prayer

He was praying in a certain place, and when he had finished, one of his disciples said to him, "Lord, teach us to pray" (Lk 11:1).

The Gospels describe Jesus spending a lot of time in prayer. "Great crowds assembled to listen to him and to be cured of their ailments, but he would withdraw to deserted places to pray" (Lk 5:15-16). "Rising very early before dawn, he left and went off to a deserted place, where he prayed" (Mk 1:35). Jesus' ministry was important, but prayer was essential, even at the cost of sleep.

On one occasion, Jesus "withdrew in a boat to a deserted place" (Mt 14:13) to pray, but was thwarted by crowds who followed him. After healing and feeding them, Jesus tried again, sending the disciples off in a boat. He then "went up on the mountain by himself to pray," and prayed until "the fourth watch of the night" (Mt 14:23, 25). The "fourth watch" ran from 3:00 to 6:00 a.m.: Jesus spent most of the night in prayer.

Jesus rose very early or stayed up very late to pray, even spending whole nights in prayer (see Lk 6:12). The disciples apparently got used to this, accounting for their behavior on several occasions. When Jesus "went up the mountain to pray" and was transfigured, Peter, James, and John slept (Lk 9:28-32). Later, Jesus went to Gethsemane to pray, and again these disciples fell asleep (see Mt 14:32-37). One Scripture scholar suggests that the disciples probably thought, "He's at it again. Another all-nighter — we might as well catch a few winks."

Yet Jesus' followers were so impressed with his prayer life that they wanted to be able to pray as he prayed. "Lord," they asked him, "teach us to pray." In response, Jesus taught them the Our Father (see Lk 11:2-4; Mt 6:9-13).

It is striking that the prayer that Jesus taught his followers is a short prayer. There are about five psalms that are as short or shorter than the Our Father, which means that about ninety-seven percent of the psalms are longer. The Lord's Prayer is one of the shortest prayers in the Bible. Nor was it accidental that Jesus taught his followers a short prayer, for he also told them, "In praying, do not babble like the pagans, who think that they will be heard because of their many words. Do not be like them" (Mt 6:7-8).

What a paradox! Jesus spent whole nights in prayer — but told his followers that long prayers were unnecessary and taught them a prayer that they could recite in twenty seconds. What's going on here?

One answer seems to be that what is important is not so much the words we use in our prayers, and certainly not the quantity of words, but rather the attitude with which we pray. Jesus taught his followers to pray to his Father as their Father. There is, in fact, good evidence that Jesus taught his followers to call upon God as *Abba*, just as he did (see Mk 14:36). When Paul writes to Greek-speaking Gentile Christians in Rome and Galatia, he reminds them that they use the Aramaic word *Abba* when they pray (see Rom 8:15; Gal 4:6).

Abba is the informal word children use to address their father. God as our *Abba* is not a distant and reserved Father, but a close and loving Father. Our *Abba* in heaven is a Father we can turn to with complete trust and confidence. Thus we do not need to multiply words when we pray: "Your Father knows what you need before you ask him" (Mt. 6:8).

That is why Jesus could spend a whole night in prayer and not need to use many words: He was in communion with his *Abba*. And that is why we do not need to ramble on endlessly when we pray: We do not need to change the mind of an aloof and uncaring God. We need only to acknowledge that God is indeed our Father and loves us; we need only to express our trust in him; we need only to enter into communion with our *Abba*.

Reminders

"In praying, do not babble like the pagans, who think that they will be heard because of their many words. Do not be like them. Your Father knows what you need before you ask him. This is how you are to pray:

Our Father in heaven,
hallowed be your name,
your kingdom come,
your will be done,
on earth as in heaven.
Give us today our daily bread;
and forgive us our debts,
as we forgive our debtors;
and do not subject us to the final test,
but deliver us from the evil one" *(Mt 6:7-13).*

If our heavenly Father knows what we need before we ask, why do we need to ask at all?

It is certainly not to nag God into doing what he is reluctant to do, nor is it to earn the favors he gives us: Jesus would say that pagans might understand prayer in such terms, but not those who have grasped what he has taught about his Father. His Father knows the things we need and will provide for us (see Mt 6:10-31). His Father even provides for those who do not deserve or acknowledge his care (see Mt 5:44-45). He is not a God who has to be talked into loving us. What then does our prayer accomplish? Let us look at the prayer Jesus taught us, and examine what we are asking for when we offer this prayer. If this is the way Jesus taught us to pray, then it must accomplish what our prayer is meant to accomplish.

The first three petitions of the Lord's Prayer are closely related. They ask God to manifest his holiness, to establish his kingdom, to accomplish his will on earth. In praying these petitions we are primarily asking God to act, rather than praying that men and women will hallow God's name, bring his kingdom, and do his will. That at least is the intent of these petitions as they are phrased in the Greek text of the Gospels. We are asking in three slightly different ways for God to complete his plan of salvation for the world. We are asking, ultimately, for the second coming of Christ.

The remaining petitions of the Lord's Prayer also have something in common: They focus on our basic individual needs. We need bread and the necessities of life each day; we need forgiveness for our sins; we need security in times of testing, and protection from evil. These are our basic needs for staying alive physically and spiritually, and we turn to God as the one who is not only able to satisfy them but, as Jesus teaches, eager to do so (see Mt 7:7-11).

But again, doesn't God know what our basic needs are before we ask? Doesn't he know that we stand in need of daily sustenance and forgiveness and protection? Of course he does. So what is the point of asking? Likewise, what is the point of asking God to complete his plan of salvation for the world? Isn't that something that he is determined to do, even apart from our asking?

We ask, not because God is absentminded and prone to forget what needs doing, but because we are absentminded and prone to forget the most important truths about the meaning of life on earth. We are all too easily caught up in the passing concerns of each day. We need regularly to remind ourselves that we are a part of God's plan to reconcile everything to himself through Jesus Christ.

If we all too easily forget the big picture, we also all too easily overlook what our basic needs really are. Our prayers of petition can become a wish list of niceties instead of focusing on what is truly important for our welfare, now and eternally. The prayer Jesus taught us draws our attention back to our basic necessities.

In praying the Lord's Prayer, we acknowledge our dependence on God to do what only God can do: complete his plan of salvation, and preserve us as a part of it. Our petitions are reminders, not to God, but to ourselves: reminders of what is truly important, reminders of what he is doing and is eager to do in our lives and in the world. In praying this prayer we add our own "Yes! Let it come to pass!" We pray that God will be God, as a reminder to ourselves that he truly is.

Daily Bread

Meanwhile, the disciples urged him, "Rabbi, eat."
But he said to them, "I have food to eat of which
you do not know." So the disciples said to one an-
other, "Could someone have brought him something
to eat?" Jesus said to them, "My food is to do the
will of the one who sent me and to finish his work"
(Jn 4:31-34).

The petition we make in the Our Father, "Give us this day our daily bread," may seem straightforward in English, but it is less so in the Greek text of the New Testament. The problem lies in a peculiar word: "Give us this day our *epiousion* bread." *Epiousion* is used by both Matthew (6:11) and Luke (11:3) to describe the bread for which we are praying, but this word is found nowhere else in the Bible, nor anywhere in all of Greek literature. Consequently, there is great uncertainty over what this rare word means.

Various ancient and modern scholars have suggested that *epiousion* might perhaps mean "for tomorrow," or perhaps "for today," or perhaps even "necessary for existence." St. Jerome, who translated the Bible into Latin, knew of the "for tomorrow" interpretation, but he translated *epiousion* into Latin either as "daily," or as *supersubstantialis* — often understood as a reference to the Eucharist.

We cannot know for certain what Matthew and Luke had in mind when they wrote *epiousion*, nor is there any way to recover the earlier Aramaic word used by Jesus when he taught the Our Father. There is therefore no reason why we should not continue to pray the Our Father as we have learned it, asking for "daily bread." On the other hand, the obscurity of this petition in the Greek New Testament can lead us to reflect on what we mean when we pray for "daily bread," and perhaps to personalize this petition in our prayer.

The word "bread" in Scripture can carry the broader meaning of food in general. Many people in this world do indeed pray for their daily bread when they get up in the morning, because having enough to eat that day is far from certain. Most of us, however, have an ample supply of groceries on hand, and for us to ask for our "daily bread" can be to acknowledge that our food and life come from God.

But the word food can also carry a broader meaning, as in Jesus' words, "My food is to do the will of the one who sent me and to finish his work" (Jn 4:34). In praying for our daily bread, we can therefore be asking for the food of doing God's will that day, for the gift of being able to serve God, for the blessing of seeing value in our work.

This is not a gift to be taken for granted. Many go off to work, or set about the duties of the day, with little more than a numb, "I gotta do this." Many have trouble seeing that what they do makes any difference for the coming of God's kingdom on earth. Most have to care for families, punch time-clocks, carry out mundane obligations. In such situations, what does it mean to ask for the daily bread of serving God?

No matter what our circumstances, we can pray that we will be God's servant in those circumstances. We might not expect to do anything different that day, but we can ask for the grace of doing it well, and the grace of recognizing how what we do is God's will for us. We can also pray that God will give us special openings to serve him, perhaps in the people we meet that day, perhaps through unexpected opportunities.

"Give us this day our daily bread" — the bread of serving God, the bread of seeing our day through his eyes, the bread of imitating Jesus, whose food was to do the will of his Father and complete his work. That is indeed food that satisfies our hunger and sustains us.

Lord, Have Mercy

Two blind men were sitting by the roadside, and when they heard that Jesus was going by, they shouted, "Lord, Son of David, have mercy on us!" The crowd rebuked them and told them to be quiet, but they shouted all the louder, "Lord, Son of David, have mercy on us!" Jesus stopped and called them. "What do you want me to do for you?" he asked. "Lord," they answered, "we want our sight." Jesus had compassion on them and touched their eyes. Immediately they received their sight and followed him (Mt 20:30-34 NIV).

Catholics of my generation remember reciting the *Kyrie eleison* at Mass, a prayer that we now pray in English as "Lord, have mercy." Although the rest of the Mass was in Latin, this prayer was recited in Greek, for *Kyrie eleison* are Greek and not Latin words.

It would be up to those who study the history of the liturgy to explain why this prayer was preserved in Greek, but one factor suggests itself: The words *Kyrie eleison* appear several times in the Gospel of Matthew, on the lips of those who are imploring Jesus for help. Those who came to Jesus spoke to him in their common language of Aramaic, but Matthew in writing his Gospel in Greek translated their words into the petition *Kyrie eleison*, "Lord, have mercy," or "Lord, have pity."

We first hear these words on the lips of the Canaanite woman whose daughter was tormented by a devil. Even though she was not Jewish, she cried out to Jesus, "Have mercy on me, Lord" (Mt 15:21-28 NIV). She persisted in her plea for mercy, eager for the crumbs that would fall from the table of Jesus, until her daughter was healed.

Likewise, the man whose son was possessed by an evil spirit that threw him into the fire also cried out to Jesus, "*Kyrie eleison*," "Lord, have mercy on my son" (Mt 17:15 NIV). The apostles had been unable to heal his son, and he turned to Jesus.

Mark records this man's anguished cry, "I do believe; help me overcome my unbelief" (Mk 9:24 NIV): I believe in you as the Lord and want to believe in you; only have mercy on my weakness of faith and have mercy on my son. Jesus did.

And the two blind men sitting by the road outside Jericho also cried out "*Kyrie eleison*," shouting to make themselves heard above the crowd, persisting in their plea for pity even when others tried to hush them. Their cry was also heard by Jesus; he healed them and they began to follow him as his disciples. Matthew presents them to us as models of discipleship: Jesus touches and restores us; we respond by following him.

In all of these instances *Kyrie eleison* was not a prayer that people recited unthinkingly and mechanically, but a cry that came from their hearts, a cry of desperate need and dependence on Jesus. Lord, have mercy, because my daughter is tormented by demons and no one else can heal her. Lord, have mercy, because we are blind and doomed to a life of begging by the side of the road unless you hear our cry and stop and touch us. Lord, have pity, for we desperately need your pity.

We, however, find it all too easy to recite the words "Lord, have mercy" at Mass without thinking too much about what we are asking for. The familiar pattern of the liturgy carries us along, whether we are conscious or not of needing the mercy of Jesus. But we desperately do need it: not perhaps at the moment for physical healing but certainly for healing from sin.

That need is the context in which we pray, "Lord, have mercy," at Mass: as a part of the penitential service, after having recalled our sins. Our cry "Lord, have mercy" is a cry for forgiveness; our plea is that Jesus would take pity on us in our sinfulness. If we were to truly acknowledge our spiritual state, our cry to him would be even more heartfelt than the cry of the Canaanite woman or the Jewish father or the two blind men.

And as in the case of the two blind men, the mercy Jesus extends to us is meant to result in our living changed lives. We cannot pray for mercy without being willing to extend mercy to others. That is the point of Jesus' parable about the two debtors (see Mt 18:23-35). Matthew uses a form of the same Greek word *eleison* in presenting Jesus' teaching: "Shouldn't you have had mercy on your fellow servant just as I had on you?" (Mt 18:35 NIV).

The mercy we ask for is the mercy we must give. Lord, have mercy — and make us merciful.

Intercessory Prayer

"Simon, Simon, Satan has asked to sift you as wheat. But I have prayed for you, Simon, that your faith may not fail. And when you have turned back, strengthen your brothers." But he replied, "Lord, I am ready to go with you to prison and to death." Jesus answered, "I tell you, Peter, before the rooster crows today, you will deny three times that you know me" (Lk 22:31-34 NIV).

There is a mystery to intercessory prayer. How can our words, our yearnings of heart, our sacrifices make a difference in what God does or in what happens to another person? How can our prayers change what God has eternally foreseen?

Some may indeed doubt that prayer makes any difference. Sometimes their skepticism stems from their own apparently unanswered prayer: "I prayed for my son, but he still left the Church." "I prayed for my wife to get well, but she died."

Yet others can attest to their prayers being answered, their intercessions being heard. They may not be able to explain how their prayers could make a difference with God or why some prayers seem to go unanswered, but they know from experience that God does hear and answer prayer.

The mystery of intercessory prayer is most apparent when our prayers are the most fervent and spring from our deepest love. We pray for people we dearly love, interceding for their well-being and health, interceding even for their relationship with God. But as we pray we are aware that God loves them with a far deeper love than we could humanly have for them. Our intercession may be little more than reminding God of how much he loves them.

Can our prayers increase God's love by one iota? Is there any need for God's love to be increased, since his love is perfect? We don't have any answers to our wondering, but we continue praying nonetheless, out of our love for the one we are praying for. We trust the instincts of our hearts more than the puzzles of our thinking.

A basic principle of the Christian life may be stated: When in doubt, look to what Jesus did, and imitate that. The Gospels present us with at least one clear case of Jesus offering up intercessory prayer for another person. During the Last Supper Jesus told Peter that he had prayed for him, that his faith might not fail. There are several striking lessons in Jesus' doing so.

First, Jesus recognized Peter as one specially favored by his Father. When Peter acknowledged Jesus to be the Christ, Jesus responded, "Blessed are you, Simon son of Jonah, for this was not revealed to you by man, but by my Father in heaven" (Mt 16:17 NIV). Yet Jesus prayed for Peter. God's love for someone, or even God's special favor for someone, does not make our prayers for that person superfluous.

Second, Jesus prayed for Peter even though he knew that Peter would deny him. Surely he must have prayed that Peter would not be put to the test or would be strong enough to surmount temptation if it was unavoidable. He urged his apostles to offer such prayer (see Lk 21:36; 22:46), and it would seem very likely that he would offer such prayer for them himself.

But Jesus knew that this prayer would not be answered, that Peter would fall. His prayer then seemed to become a prayer that Peter's fall would not destroy his faith and that Peter would recover from it and be able to strengthen the other apostles.

If we are right in believing that Jesus prayed that Peter would not fall, then we have a case of even Jesus' intercessory prayer apparently not being answered. If there is a mystery to our intercessory prayer, there is a far greater mystery to the intercessory prayer of Jesus!

Third, the most simple, definite, and certain lesson from this passage is the need for and legitimacy of intercessory prayer. Whatever mysteries there may be about it, Jesus prayed for Peter. Whatever mysteries there may be to our own intercessory prayer, we are on solid ground in imitating the example of Jesus. Jesus prayed for Peter. We too are to pray for those we love.

Confidence in Prayer

"Suppose one of you has a friend to whom he goes at midnight and says, 'Friend, lend me three loaves of bread, for a friend of mine has arrived at my house from a journey and I have nothing to offer him,' and he says in reply from within, 'Do not bother me; the door has already been locked and my children and I are already in bed. I cannot get up to give you anything.' I tell you, if he does not get up to give him the loaves because of their friendship, he will get up to give him whatever he needs because of his persistence" (Lk 11:5-8).

Jesus based his parables on the life experiences of his original listeners. Because our culture is different from the culture in which Jesus lived, we have to make some mental adjustments as we read the parables.

Have any of us ever been awakened at midnight by a man wanting three loaves of bread? Probably not. Were we, we might tell him that that is what 7-Elevens are for.

But there were no twenty-four-hour convenience stores in the time of Jesus. Each family baked its own bread, perhaps several days' supply at a time. A family who had run out of bread might know a neighbor who had some left over.

There were no Holiday Inns either, and travelers stayed with friends or relatives. Even when guests arrived unexpectedly, hospitality was an almost sacred duty. One might even have to wake up a neighbor to help out.

More realistically, one might have to wake up a neighbor's

whole family, since ordinary houses had but a single room for living and sleeping. A man was asleep on a mat on the floor, his family sleeping around him, when a friend awakened him to ask for bread. Jesus asks his listeners to imagine the man's response to such a request.

In the culture of Jesus' time, the man would, of course, get up and give bread to his friend, even though it meant waking his family. To turn down a request to help a guest would have been shameful, for the duty of hospitality fell on the whole village. The family could get back to sleep again, but to refuse bread for a guest in the village would bring dishonor in a culture that prized honor.

We often miss this implication of the parable because a key word in verse eight is usually translated as the "persistence" — the persistence of the friend asking for bread. But Kenneth Bailey, a scholar who studied the parables against the backdrop of village life, notes that the Greek word translated as "persistence" literally means "shamelessness." Furthermore, this "shamelessness" refers not to the friend asking for bread, but to the man who was awakened, and it has the sense of avoiding shameful conduct. The parable does not have to do with persistence in asking, but with a request being granted because turning it down would be dishonorable.

Jesus told this as a parable about prayer. It has been understood to teach the importance of persistence in prayer, much as does the parable of the corrupt judge and the persistent widow (see Lk 18:1-8). But Bailey suggests a different interpretation. Jesus' first listeners would have found it unthinkable that anyone would turn down a request, even if inconvenient, for bread for a guest. If such a request was not granted out of friendship, it certainly would be granted to avoid the loss of honor that denying it would entail. And if one could be confident of a neighbor's meeting one's needs for the sake of honor, how much more confident can one be when approaching God?

In favor of this interpretation are the words of Jesus four verses later, which draw a similar lesson: "If you, then, who are wicked, know how to give good gifts to your children, how much more will the Father in heaven give the holy Spirit to those who ask him?" (Lk 11:13). We can pray with great confidence, for God is far more responsive to us than we are to our friends and children.

Abba, Father

He took with him Peter, James, and John, and began to be troubled and distressed. Then he said to them, "My soul is sorrowful even to death. Remain here and keep watch." He advanced a little and fell to the ground and prayed that if it were possible the hour might pass by him; he said, "Abba, Father, all things are possible to you. Take this cup away from me, but not what I will but what you will" (Mk 14:33-36).

Jesus taught us to pray to our heavenly Father with confidence and even intimacy. He knows our needs before we ask (see Mt 6:8); he loves us far more than we love our own children (see Mt 7:11). Jesus authorized us to approach his Father as our Father, crying out "Abba, Father" (Rom 8:15; Gal 4:6).

But what about those times when God seems distant or absent from our lives? When everything seems to be going wrong, and we have a hard time stirring up any conviction that God cares for us? When words of prayer stick dry in our throats?

Not every Christian may experience such times, but a good many do. The causes can be manifold. Physical and emotional fatigue can numb us; bouts of depression can send us careening toward despair. Illness may sap our spiritual as well as physical strength. And of course, our sins take their toll.

Whatever the specific causes might be, the end results may be the same: We lack a sense of intimacy with God; we have little conviction that he is caring for us; we find it very difficult to pray. We may know that our feelings are an unreliable guide in spiritual matters. We may know that God loves us no matter how we feel, and cares for us no matter the mess we are in. But what we know in our head has a hard time making it into our hearts and onto our tongues; our prayer remains barren.

Jesus gave us an example of how we should pray when we find ourselves in such a state. He taught by example even when it came to anguished prayer.

Consider what was on Jesus' mind the night before he died. He knew that suffering and a horrible death awaited him. He knew that his closest friends would betray, deny, abandon him. He experienced the same turmoil of emotions that we would in such circumstances. He was "troubled and distressed"; he was "sorrowful even to death" (Mk 14:33, 34). He "was in such agony and he prayed so fervently that his sweat became like drops of blood falling on the ground" (Lk 22:44).

On previous occasions, Jesus' prayers had been answered with reassuring words from heaven (see Lk 3:21-22; 9:28-35). But in his hour of anguish, no voice proclaimed, "You are my beloved son; with you I am well pleased" (Mk 1:11). There was only silence and darkness, and the snores of Jesus' friends.

How could Jesus have confidence in a God who would let him suffer and die? How could Jesus pray with intimacy to a God who made no response? What words of prayer could be used in a time of such great distress?

Jesus used the words, "Abba, Father . . . not what I will but what you will" (Mk 14:36). Even in his hour of greatest anguish, Jesus called upon God as his Abba, his loving Father. Even when faced with suffering and death, Jesus entrusted himself into his Father's hands.

And that is how he taught us to pray, no matter how we feel, no matter what the circumstances. "This is how you are to pray: Our Father in heaven . . . your will be done" (Mt 6:9, 10). Even in the most extreme circumstances, even when we least feel like it, we are to pray to God as our loving Father and commit ourselves into his care for us. That is how Jesus prayed, even in his darkest hour. That is how we are to pray, no matter the darkness.

Thy Will Be Done

Mary said, "Behold, I am the handmaid of the Lord. May it be done to me according to your word" (Lk 1:38).

He advanced a little and fell prostrate in prayer, saying, "My Father, if it is possible, let this cup pass from me; yet, not as I will, but as you will." Withdrawing a second time, he prayed again, "My Father, if it is not possible that this cup pass without my drinking it, your will be done!" He left them and withdrew again and prayed a third time, saying the same thing again (Mt 26:39, 42, 44).

If we had to choose the most decisive turning point in the life of Mary, we would have to select the Annunciation, when Gabriel told her that she had been chosen to be the mother of the Son of God. Before that moment she had been, to all outward appearances, merely a young girl who lived in the small village of Nazareth and who loved God with her whole heart and soul. After the Annunciation, after the power of the Holy Spirit overshadowed her, she was the *Theotokos*, the God-bearer, the mother of God.

But God does not force himself into anyone's life, and Mary had to freely accept that to which God called her. Her initial reaction to Gabriel's message was one of consternation: "She was greatly troubled at what was said and pondered what sort of greeting this might be" (Lk 1:29). Even Gabriel's promise that she would bear the Son of the Most High raised questions for her: "How can this be, since I have no relations with a man?"

(Lk 1:34). Her reactions are entirely understandable: What would be our astonishment if an angel stood before us, and promised a miracle beyond imagining in our lives? Yet despite her surprise and astonishment, she accepted God's invitation and will for her.

Jesus likewise faced many moments of decision in his life: Even though he was the Son of God, he was also fully human, and he had to chart the course of his life by the decisions he made. On the eve of his public ministry he faced the temptations of Satan to use his power for his own glory. Later he had to decide whether he would be the kind of messiah that the crowds clamored for (see Jn 6:15), or the kind of messiah that the crowds would turn against and crucify.

The most crucial moment of decision came for Jesus after the Last Supper, at the foot of the Mount of Olives. Jesus knew that Judas had betrayed him and at that very moment was probably leading an armed band to the Garden of Gethsemane, knowing it to be Jesus' favorite place of prayer (see Lk 22:39-40). Jesus also knew what the outcome would be if he was arrested: He knew that his enemies plotted his death, and that it would be an agonizing and humiliating one. Yet escape was still possible: A quick ten-minute hike would take him up and over the Mount of Olives and into the Judean wilderness which began on its eastern slopes. At night no one would find him there.

But Jesus also knew what his Father asked of him, and in prayer he embraced his Father's will, despite what he knew it would cost him. He had no attraction to dying; he knew the cruelties of public execution, and his flesh rebelled at the thought of what lay ahead. Yet at this, the most crucial moment of decision in his life, he prayed, "Your will be done," and waited for Judas and the mob to find him.

Jesus also taught us to pray, "Your will be done." We echo his words every time we pray the Our Father. Rarely do we pray these words with the anguish with which Jesus prayed them in Gethsemane; rarely do we use them to commit ourselves so wholeheartedly to God's will for us. Most of our days, and most of our prayers, are uneventful — the simple living out of a course already chosen.

Yet the deepest meaning of these words that Jesus taught us to pray are to be found at moments of decision, when the course of our life does hang in the balance. Which path should we take? Will we allow God's will to be done in our lives, even though we know that it will be at great cost to us? Will we, like Mary, embrace God's invitation to us, forever altering who we are? Will we, like her, entrust ourselves to God as his handmaids and servants, allowing him to use us however he decides? Will we, like Jesus, accept the cup that our Father offers us, no matter how bitter it may seem? Will we pray from the depths of our being, "Your will be done"?

6

Living as Disciples

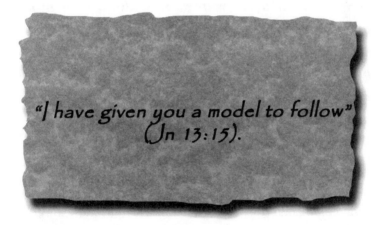

"I have given you a model to follow"
(Jn 13:15).

Loving God

One of the scribes, when he came forward and heard them disputing and saw how well he had answered them, asked him, "Which is the first of all the commandments?" Jesus replied, "The first is this: 'Hear, O Israel! The Lord our God is Lord alone! You shall love the Lord your God with all your heart, with all your soul, with all your mind, and with all your strength.' The second is this: 'You shall love your neighbor as yourself.' There is no other commandment greater than these" (Mk 12:28-31).

Loving another person as much as we love ourselves is not easy: We have a deeply ingrained inclination to prefer the best for ourselves. If Jesus had given us only the second of the two great commandments, we would still have our life's work cut out for us. But the second great commandment is only the second, and the first great commandment is even more demanding.

How do we go about loving God? As a starting point, we can consider how we love another person. Just as God compares his love to human love (see Is 49:15, 62:5; Mt 7:9-11), so, too, we can get some insight into the way we are to love God by reflecting on how we love those most dear to us: parents, spouse, children, close friends.

One way we express our love for them is by serving their needs, performing acts of kindness, doing the things that make them happy. We likewise express our love for God through the various ways we serve him and the coming of his kingdom.

But while service of God can be done out of love, it is not identical with love of God. Paul writes that it is possible to give away everything we own, even our bodies, but do so without love (see 1 Cor 13:3). It is possible to spend our lives serving God without really loving him very much. We may be like the prodigal son's older brother, who could tell his father, "'Look, all these years I served you and not once did I disobey your orders" (Lk 15:29), yet seemed to have little closeness to his father.

What then does love for another mean? Being with and speaking with a beloved is certainly essential. The poetry of love is filled with images of longing to be with the beloved, longing to hear the beloved's voice, longing to gaze into the beloved's eyes. The amount of time two newly-in-love people may spend just being together seems limitless.

At the sight of young lovers, older heads may shake knowingly, "They will get over it." And indeed they may. But shouldn't some of their first-love enthusiasm mark our love for God? Shouldn't our love for God be expressed by wanting to be in his presence and conversing with him in prayer? Brother Lawrence, a seventeenth-century Carmelite, said, "We should establish ourselves in the presence of God, talking always with him; it is an infamous thing to leave his presence to engage in follies."

For most of us, entering into the presence of God is something we strive to do a few times in the course of a day; the rest of our time is taken up with the myriad concerns of our lives. We can intend to do all we do for God, but our minds are on what we are doing, not on God. And if we are honest, we recognize that we are not doing all but only some for God: Much is for ourselves.

Yet Jesus tells us that we are to love God with *all* our heart, with *all* our soul, with *all* our mind, with *all* our strength. It is the *alls* that seem impossible. To expend our strength and efforts only for God, to have our minds set only on God, to have hearts aflame with love for God: Few of us have achieved what Jesus commands.

We must therefore come before God and admit that we fall far short of living up to the great commandment, and ask for the grace of doing so. "God, let me fall in love with you."

How Talented Are You?

"A man who was going on a journey called in his servants and entrusted his possessions to them. To one he gave five talents; to another, two; to a third, one — to each according to his ability" (Mt 25:14-15).

Are you a one-talent person, a three-talent person, or a five-talent person?

And what's a talent, anyway?

Originally, a talent was a weight of precious metal — say, sixty-five pounds of gold. In Jesus' parable, talents represented large amounts of money that a man entrusted to his servants to manage in his absence. Eventually, the word "talent" took on the meaning of the gifts and abilities with which we are endowed.

The point of Jesus' parable was not simply that we ought to use our God-given gifts and abilities to their fullest. The context in which Jesus told this parable makes it clear that he had a more specific message in mind. Chapters 24 and 25 of Matthew's Gospel are a unified block of teaching, devoted to the end of this age (see Mt 24:3). Jesus addresses the question of when it will happen, but for the most part he speaks about what we should do while awaiting his return.

Jesus holds up the example of a "faithful and prudent servant, whom the master has put in charge of his household to distribute to them their food at the proper time" (Mt 24:45). The disciples of Jesus are likewise to be faithful in carrying out the responsibilities he has given them, until he returns. Jesus might not return as soon as they expect, and they must be prudently prepared for this possibility — the point of the parable of the ten bridesmaids (see Mt 25:1-13).

What are the responsibilities Jesus gives to his disciples? Jesus concludes his discourse with a Last Judgment scene. Then he will say to his faithful and prudent servants "I was hungry and you gave me food, I was thirsty and you gave me drink. . . . Whatever you did for one of these least brothers of mine, you did for me" (Mt 25:35, 40). Caring for those in need is a high-priority responsibility for Jesus' followers, as they await his return.

This is the context in which Jesus tells the parable of the talents (see Mt 25:14-30). Every follower of Jesus has been given certain abilities, gifts, resources, charisms, skills, aptitudes: Our talents come in a wide variety of colors and sizes. Some of us may be more gifted than others: There may be one-talent disciples and three-talent disciples and five-talent disciples. But no disciple of Jesus is completely ungifted. Every follower of Jesus is equipped in one way or another to be a "faithful and prudent servant" who distributes food to the hungry, or solace to the mourning, or justice to the wronged. Every one of us is equipped in some way to be commended by Jesus at the Last Judgment for having served him in the least of his brothers and sisters.

The question each of us must ask ourselves is, therefore, "What are my talents?" How have I been equipped and gifted to serve Jesus? What are the one, three, or five abilities that I have been entrusted with so that I may use them in the service of others? How well am I using them? It might not be a bad idea to make a list of your talents, and periodically review how you are using them as an examination of conscience.

It doesn't matter whether we have one talent or five talents: The number of talents we have been given is God's responsibility, not ours. Nor does it matter all that much whether our talents equip us to do mighty works or only modest deeds: That too is in God's hands. What does matter is what we do with what we have been given. That matters eternally — as Jesus' description of the Last Judgment makes clear.

Have We Left All?

Peter began to say to him, "Look, we have left
everything and followed you" (Mk 10:28 NRSV).

It is not easy to leave everything in order to follow Jesus. Peter
thought that he and the other apostles had left all for Jesus'
sake, but the Gospels indicate that the matter was not that
simple.

We usually use Peter's assertion that they had left all as the
key for interpreting passages such as Luke 5:11, which seemingly portray the apostles abandoning their fishing businesses
for Jesus: "When they had brought their boats to shore, they
left everything and followed him" (NRSV). But John portrays
Peter and other apostles doing commercial fishing even after
Jesus' resurrection (see Jn 21:1-14). And there always seemed
to be a boat at hand whenever Jesus wished to cross the Sea of
Galilee. Perhaps the apostles did not leave their businesses so
much as take leaves of absence to travel with Jesus. After all,
they still had families to support. However, the Gospels do not
tell us enough to resolve the matter with certainty.

There are other and more important considerations than
whether the apostles left all their possessions. The apostles did
not leave all personal ambitions behind when they followed
Jesus. James and John wanted to be given the two chief positions of honor and power by Jesus (see Mk 10:35-37), which
upset the other ten apostles, who wanted a shot at these positions themselves (note Jesus' correction of the other ten in Mk
10:41-45). Luke presents us with the apostles repeatedly arguing among themselves over who was greatest — even during
the Last Supper (see Lk 9:46; 22:24). Even their "leaving all"
led to their wondering what they would thereby gain: "We have
left everything and followed you. What then will we have?"

(Mt 19:27 NRSV). Better for them to have left their self-seeking ambition behind rather than their nets when they set out to follow Jesus.

Nor did they leave their fears behind. They were frightened during a storm at sea with Jesus in the boat (see Mk 4:36-41) — and then frightened again a second time in a similar situation (see Mk 6:50). In the moment of crisis, all of them fled, and Peter denied he even knew Jesus. After Jesus' resurrection, they hid out of fear (see Jn 20:19), even though Mary Magdalene had told them of seeing the risen Lord (see John 20:18).

There is much else that the apostles did not leave behind when they "left all" to follow Jesus: their slowness to understand Jesus and put their absolute trust in him; their ill-tempers (see Lk 9:52-55; Mk 3:17); their narrowness (see Mk 10:38); their reluctance to embrace the cross. But the Gospel accounts of the apostles were not written so that we could compile a catalog of their failings; they were written as examples and warnings to us, to lead us to self-examination.

Have we left all to follow Jesus?

We can perhaps look back on a moment when we made a conscious decision to give our lives to Jesus and accept him as our Lord and Savior. Or we might remember a moment when we were washed over by a flood of grace and decided to love God with our whole heart and soul, and to spend our lives in his service. Such moments are important — but more important is how we live them out. We cannot answer the question "Have we left all?" simply by looking back on a decision we made; we must look at how we live each day, and examine whether we have in fact left all.

We may have once decided to give ourselves completely to the Lord — but, consciously or unconsciously, we may have taken back part of what we had once given him. Or we may have given ourselves as completely to Jesus Christ as we were capable of doing at the moment of our decision, but not touched the depths of our selves. There may be more that Jesus invites us to now give him, that we were incapable of freely giving him in the past.

To leave all to follow Jesus may be like peeling an onion. We peel away all the sin and encumbrances that we can see, and we think we have gotten rid of everything — but there is another layer beneath, a layer we could not see because the first layer hid it. We cannot simply say, "I have peeled away everything for Jesus." We must instead look at ourselves anew, and peel away again, as painful as that might be. To give Jesus everything is a process, not a onetime achievement.

Peter's Refusal, Jesus' Demand

So he got up from the meal, took off his outer clothing, and wrapped a towel around his waist. After that, he poured water into a basin and began to wash his disciples' feet, drying them with the towel that was wrapped around him. He came to Simon Peter, who said to him, "Lord, are you going to wash my feet?" Jesus replied, "You do not realize now what I am doing, but later you will understand." "No, said Peter. "you shall never wash my feet." Jesus answered, "Unless I wash you, you have no part with me" (Jn 13:4-8 NIV).

After Jesus finished washing his followers' feet, he explained the meaning of his action: "Now that I, your Lord and Teacher, have washed your feet, you also should wash one another's feet. I have set you an example that you should do as I have done for you" (Jn 13:14-15 NIV). The basic message is clear enough to us, even if we do not find it easy to imitate the pattern set by Christ.

But there is one detail about this passage in Scripture that may still perplex us. When Peter refuses to let Jesus wash his feet, Jesus tells him, "Unless I wash you, you have no part with me" (Jn 13:8 NIV). Other translations render this verse "you have nothing in common with me" or "you will have no share in my heritage." This is a very strong statement! Jesus makes Peter's salvation depend on his allowing Jesus to wash his feet. If Peter refuses, he will be completely cut off from the life that Jesus came to bring.

We may wonder why Jesus said this to Peter. After all, Peter's reaction to the thought of Jesus' washing his feet was very natural and understandable. The duty of washing feet was usually left to household slaves, and rabbinic law even exempted Jewish slaves from such service. A disciple might wash his teacher's feet as a sign of respect, but Jesus seemed rather to be putting himself in the role of a slave: The towel wrapped around one's waist was the characteristic garb of servants or slaves. No wonder Peter rebelled at the idea of Jesus washing his feet. Would we have reacted any differently?

But despite the fact that Peter's reaction was a very natural one, Jesus demanded to wash his feet, and made his demand very absolute: "Unless I wash you, you have no part with me." Why did Jesus demand this of Peter? And equally importantly, what does this demand mean for us?

Jesus might have meant this as a lesson in the importance of being served. Our instincts of independence rebel against being in debt to someone else. We might rather do without than to have to receive from another. But our eternal salvation is something that we cannot achieve on our own and must be willing to accept. Our pride and independence must not be allowed to stand in the way of receiving life from Christ. We must be willing to let him serve us, on his terms.

Further, Jesus demanded that his disciples imitate him. We (and Peter) might prefer that he did not go to the extremes he did in serving us, because we know that we, in turn, are called to go to the same lengths. We might rebel at the thought of Jesus washing our feet because that means we must wash the feet of each other. It would be much easier to imitate Christ if his love were less generous and self-sacrificing.

There is perhaps still another level of meaning in this scene. Does John intend us to understand a reference to the waters of baptism in this passage? If so, then the link with eternal life becomes quite appropriate: "Unless I wash [baptize] you, you have no part [inheritance] with me." This demands that we accept Jesus as the source of life, as the one who saves us by incorporating us in himself. In baptism we receive the life of Christ; to refuse Jesus is to refuse eternal life.

The demand Jesus made of Peter is not an enigma to be solved like a crossword puzzle, but rather a mystery for our meditation. It can be the springboard for our asking Jesus: What do you demand of me? What do you ask me to receive from you? What do you ask me to do in imitation of you? How do you invite me to receive and grow in eternal life?

Eye for Eye, Tooth for Tooth

"You have heard that it was said, 'Eye for eye, and tooth for tooth.' but I tell you, Do not resist an evil person. If someone strikes you on the right cheek, turn to him the other also. . . . I tell you: Love your enemies and pray for those who persecute you" *(Mt 5:38-39, 44 NIV).*

We sometimes think that "an eye for an eye, a tooth for a tooth" is the law of the jungle, but it is not. The law of the jungle is better expressed in Lamech's evil boast early in the book of Genesis: "I have killed a man for wounding me, a young man for injuring me. If Cain is avenged seven times, then Lamech seventy-seven times" (Gn 4:23-24 NIV). It was precisely to limit such massive retaliation that the law of Moses prescribed that the punishment inflicted could be no worse than the original injury: "If anyone injures his neighbor, whatever he has done must be done to him: fracture for fracture, eye for eye, tooth for tooth" (Lv 24:19-20 NIV).

But even though this commandment limited retaliation, it could not prevent an endless cycle of retaliation giving rise to counter-retaliation. When people took justice into their own hands it was easy for feuds between individuals or families to develop. And after several rounds of retaliation and counter-retaliation, the original cause of the feud could well be forgotten, and yet the feud continue, feeding on itself. It was to forestall an endless cycle of vengeance killing arising from one person accidentally killing another that "cities of refuge" were prescribed. They were places where anyone who had accidentally caused the death of another could be safe from those who would otherwise exact blood vengeance (see Nm 35:6-28).

When Jesus proclaimed his new law in the Sermon on the Mount, he addressed some of the same basic situations as the law of Moses. Jesus commands his followers to break the cycle of violence by not returning evil for evil. Even if we are tempted to dismiss his command as "impractical," there is yet a strand of utter realism within it. If we have enemies, then we are most likely also someone else's enemy. And just as we might consider ourselves the innocent party being wronged by them, so they may consider themselves the innocent party being wronged by us. As long as each of us demands an eye for an eye and tooth for a tooth, the conflict will continue endlessly. Only when one side — or ideally both sides — gives up its eye-for-an-eye demand will the cycle of hatred be broken.

Jesus asks his followers to take the first step. We are not to return evil for what we perceive (rightly or wrongly) to be evil. We are to love our enemies — who by definition are the people that we otherwise would not love.

Our actions are furthermore to be not merely external actions that we do only because Jesus makes us, but are to flow from and give rise to an inner attitude of forgiveness. It is only a few verses later in Matthew's account of the Sermon on the Mount that Jesus teaches his followers to pray the Our Father. The prayer includes the petition "Forgive us our debts, as we also have forgiven our debtors" (Mt 6:12 NIV). Jesus then highlights this verse of the Our Father: "For if you forgive men when they sin against you, your heavenly Father will also forgive you" (Mt 6:14-15 NIV). If we demand a tooth for a tooth from others, so will it be demanded of us.

Granted that our forgiveness and turning the other cheek might break the cycle of hatred and retaliation — won't others take advantage of us? Quite possibly so. They certainly did of Jesus: They nailed him to a cross. But his call to discipleship is a call to suffer his fate: "If anyone would come after me, he must deny himself and take up his cross and follow me" (Mt 16:24 NIV). We have to shoulder the cross to live according Jesus' teachings.

Barriers or Helpers?

... As he was leaving Jericho with his disciples and a sizable crowd, Bartimaeus, a blind man, the son of Timaeus, sat by the roadside begging. On hearing that it was Jesus of Nazareth, he began to cry out and say, "Jesus, son of David, have pity on me." And many rebuked him, telling him to be silent. But he kept calling out all the more, "Son of David, have pity on me." Jesus stopped and said, "Call him." So they called the blind man, saying to him, "Take courage; get up, he is calling you." He threw aside his cloak, sprang up, and came to Jesus (Mk 10:46-50).

When we read this passage, our attention is usually focused on Jesus or on Bartimaeus. But the behavior of Jesus' followers is worth noting. As they are walking with Jesus, they hear a blind beggar cry out for Jesus' mercy — and they tell him to shut up! Is that any way for followers of Jesus to act? Why would they hinder someone from coming to Jesus and receiving his mercy?

This wasn't the first time the disciples tried to prevent others from coming to Jesus. In fact, a similar scene occurs earlier in the same chapter of Mark's Gospel: "And people were bringing children to him that he might touch them, but the disciples rebuked them. When Jesus saw this he became indignant and said to them, 'Let the children come to me; do not prevent them' " (Mk 10:13-14). The disciples apparently did not learn a lesson from this, for it is not long before they rebuke Bartimaeus just as they had rebuked the parents bringing their children to Jesus.

Why were the disciples intent on shielding Jesus from children and beggars? Did they have a mistaken notion of the respect due Jesus, and want to keep noisy children and dirty beggars at a distance? Did they want to hog Jesus' mercy and not share it with others? Did they want to reserve discipleship for people like themselves, and exclude certain others as undesirables?

The Gospels don't spell out the disciples' motives, so we can only speculate. One way of speculating might be to ask ourselves, "Do I see anything of myself in the first disciples turning people away? Are there those whom I hesitate to welcome as disciples of Jesus? What is the source of my own hesitations and narrowness?" Perhaps we behave much like the first disciples behaved, and for the same reasons.

There is a happy ending to the Bartimaeus story, however, for Jesus' disciples had an apparent change of heart. After Jesus told his followers to call Bartimaeus to him, they did so without sulking. They said to Bartimaeus, "Take courage; get up, he is calling you" (Mk 10:49).

Their words exhibit the essence of evangelism: proclaiming to others that Jesus is calling them, and that they can approach him without fear. Since Bartimaeus was blind, the disciples probably had to lend a hand and guide him to Jesus. Through their help, Bartimaeus was able to come into the presence of Jesus, receive his mercy, be healed of his blindness, and become a disciple.

We have two basic options: We can be barriers or helpers.

We can act like the disciples acted toward the children and as they initially acted toward Bartimaeus: We can be indifferent or even hostile toward others who are in need of Jesus, and be barriers keeping them from Jesus.

Or we can behave as the disciples finally behaved toward Bartimaeus: encouraging him to approach Jesus, assuring him that Jesus was calling him, guiding his steps toward Jesus. We can help others experience Jesus' mercy and become his disciples.

Which are we doing?

In Memory of Him

Then he took the bread, said the blessing, broke it, and gave it to them, saying, "This is my body, which will be given for you; do this in memory of me." And likewise the cup after they had eaten, saying, "This cup is the new covenant in my blood, which will be shed for you" (Lk 22:19-20).

Jesus' command at the Last Supper, "Do this in memory of me," is the most solemn of his instructions to us. The setting alone guarantees its importance: Jesus is eating a last meal with his closest followers on the night before he is to die. What he says and does are his final instruction and testimony — his last will and testament, as it were.

Since "Do this in memory of me" is such an important command, we should ask: What is included in the "this" that we are to do in memory of Jesus?

The most obvious meaning is that the Church is to celebrate the Eucharist, offering bread and wine that become the body and blood of Christ. Catholics take Jesus very literally when he proclaims, "This is my body; this is my blood." In the words of the new *Catechism*, "In the Eucharist Christ gives us the very body which he gave up for us on the cross, the very blood which he 'poured out for many for the forgiveness of sins' " (CCC 1365). Any understanding of Jesus' command, "Do this in memory of me," must start with the Eucharist.

But "Do this in memory of me" was not the only command of Jesus at the Last Supper, and his other commands throw light on the implications of the Eucharist.

In Luke's Gospel, just after instituting the Eucharist, Jesus tells his followers, "Let the greatest among you be as the youngest, and the leader as the servant. For who is greater: the one seated at table or the one who serves? Is it not the one seated at table? I am among you as the one who serves" (Lk 22:26, 27; see also Mk 10:45: "The Son of Man did not come to be served but to serve and to give his life as a ransom for many"). Jesus' giving up of himself on the cross was the fulfillment of a life of service. His followers were also to do that in memory of him: They were to serve as he served, laying down their lives for one another.

This is made clear in John's account of the Last Supper. John tells us that Jesus washed his disciples' feet and then said to them, "I have given you a model to follow, so that as I have done for you, you should also do" (Jn 13:15). Jesus' command at the Last Supper was, "As I have loved you, so you also should love one another" (Jn 13:34). Loving others as Jesus has loved us — washing another's feet in whatever form it is needed — also falls under the heading of doing in memory of Jesus.

At the Last Supper, Jesus did not merely give his followers bread and wine as his body and blood, but bread as his body "which will be given for you" and wine as his blood "which will be shed for you." To receive the Eucharist is not to receive the body and blood of someone who died in a boating accident on the Sea of Galilee, but to receive him who gave himself up to be crucified for our sake. And that enters into the meaning of his command, "Do this in memory of me." We are to imitate not only what Jesus did while reclining at the Last Supper, but also what he did on the cross, in culmination of a lifetime of self-giving. We are to love as he loved, all day, every day.

I have sometimes thought that Mass ended too quickly after Communion — that we had barely received the Eucharist when we were on our way out the door, heading back to our homes or jobs. But perhaps that is as it should be: Receiving the body and blood of Christ is not the end but the foundation and beginning of what we do in memory of him.

Feed My Sheep — Follow Me

"Do you love me? . . . Feed my sheep. Very truly, I tell you, when you were younger, you used to fasten your own belt and to go wherever you wished. But when you grow old, you will stretch out your hands, and someone else will fasten a belt around you and take you where you do not wish to go." (He said this to indicate the kind of death by which he would glorify God.) After this he said to him, "Follow me" (Jn 21:17-19 NRSV).

Jesus' last invitation to Peter echoes his first: "Follow me" (see Mk 1:16-18). The last invitation is charged with more meaning than the first, for much has happened in between — particularly the crucifixion and resurrection of Jesus. When Peter first began following Jesus, he was following him into the unknown. Now when Jesus invites Peter to follow him, it is an invitation to the cross.

Jesus apparently quotes a popular proverb observing that, while the young can dress themselves and go about as they want, the elderly may be dependent on others for help in getting dressed and going places. Jesus gives this proverb a deeper meaning, making it an allusion to the kind of death Peter will suffer. When Peter is old, his arms will be stretched out and tied to the crossbeam of a cross, and Peter will be led away to be crucified.

John's Gospel calls Peter's death the means by which he will glorify God. Jesus uses similar language for his own crucifixion: It is his hour of glorification (see Jn 12:23-24). In the context of speaking about his death, Jesus proclaimed, "Whoever serves me must follow me" (Jn 12:26 NRSV). Now when Jesus asks Peter to serve him (to feed his sheep) and to follow him, he is inviting Peter to the cross. Peter's service as the shepherd of Jesus' flock will result in his crucifixion in Rome by Nero.

What of us who will not glorify God by suffering death as a martyr? What meaning do Jesus' words to Peter have for us?

On the human level, some of us may experience the truth of the proverb Jesus quotes. We will get old and may need help getting dressed; we may find ourselves in a nursing home when we would rather be living in our own house or apartment. It will be a time when our only recourse will be to embrace the mystery of the cross and believe that following Jesus leads to eternal life, even if our following is now but a slow shuffle.

Even if we are blessed with good health to the end of our lives, Jesus' words can carry meaning for us. Jesus asked Peter to serve him by feeding his sheep; Jesus likewise asks us to serve him, and he has given each of us a particular way of doing so. There are all kinds of sheep and all kinds of hunger; there are all sorts of ways in which we may feed them. Jesus talked about our abilities to serve in his parable of the talents (see Mt 25:14-30); Paul speaks of much the same thing in his discussion of the gifts of the Spirit (see 1 Cor 12-14).

To persevere in our service of Jesus, in our use of our talents and gifts and opportunities, can mean following Jesus along the Way of the Cross. When we were young we might have had many choices, but committed ourselves to a certain path or a particular form of service. Now it may be old hat for us, or even a little stale and confining. But we may know that the way in which we are able to glorify God is through remaining faithful to our service, even bound to our service like Peter will be bound to the cross, for the sheep we are feeding are still hungry. Jesus still asks us, "Do you love me?"; Jesus still invites us, "Feed my sheep — and follow me."

7

Looking Behind the Words

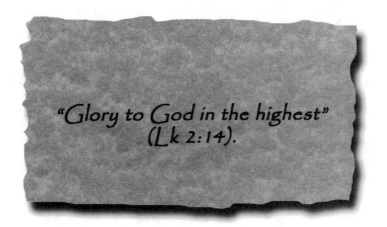

"Glory to God in the highest"
(Lk 2:14).

Glory to God in the Highest

"Glory to God in the highest
and on earth peace to those on whom his favor
rests" (Lk 2:14).

Sometimes very familiar biblical phrases harbor unsuspected meaning. We think we know what they mean, but then one day discover that their meaning is different or deeper than we had realized.

One candidate for unsuspected meaning is the hymn the angels sang at the birth of Jesus, a hymn that gives us the beginning of the Gloria we recite at Sunday Mass: "Glory to God in the highest, and peace to his people on earth."

What does it mean to give glory to God "in the highest"? Does this mean to give in the highest form of glory — perhaps our most heartfelt and exuberant praise? While this might be a possible interpretation of the phrase, it is not its meaning in the Gospel of Luke.

The Greek text of Luke literally reads, "Glory in highest to God." Scholars agree that the meaning is "glory in highest heaven to God." Greek sometimes uses adjectives to imply the noun they modify. For example, when we pray in the Our Father, "deliver us from evil," the implied meaning in Greek is "deliver us from the evil one" — that is, Satan.

In the angels' praise it is implied that the "highest" in which is God's glory is the highest heaven. This echoes other biblical texts: for example, the first verse of Psalm 148, "Praise the Lord from the heavens; / give praise in the heights." The Greek translation of this psalm uses the same word for "heights" that in Luke's Gospel we find translated as "highest."

So what are we really saying when we recite the Gloria? We are acknowledging the glory that is God's in heaven, and in

that acknowledgment we too are glorifying him. We are joining ourselves to a heavenly chorus of praise, the kind we are
given a glimpse of in the book of Revelation (see Rv 7:11-12,
for example). It is not that we give God our highest praise (although that is good to do), but that we do our tiny part to join
in and say "yes" to the glory he has in heaven.

The second phrase on the angels' lips may also have its surprise for us. Catholic translations of Scripture used to render it,
"and on earth peace among men of good will." Protestants traditionally understood this phrase to mean "and on earth peace,
good will toward men." Today both Catholic and Protestant Scripture scholars generally agree that the real meaning of the Greek
text is "and on earth peace to those on whom his favor rests."

There is a parallelism in the angels' prayer: glory in heaven
to God, peace on earth to God's people — that is, peace to
those whom he has favored by sending his Son so that they
might become his people. God's gift of peace is not a reward
for our "good will" either toward God or toward one another. It
is foremost a result of God's good will and favor toward us.

In the Gloria we pray a shortened version of the angels'
words: "and peace to his people on earth." In praying this we
should remember the basis of peace on earth, a basis that was
explicit in the angels' praise. Peace is the gift of Christ to us
(see Jn 20:19, 21, 26), given to us (as are all things we receive
in Christ) because of God's love for us.

Should we feel abashed if we have been missing some of
the meaning of biblical texts, or praying prayers without knowing precisely what we are saying? I do not think so. There is so
much more meaning in Scripture than we will ever discover,
even with a lifetime of study, that I do not think God will hold
our relative ignorance against us. He listens to our hearts when
we pray: He doesn't try to pick apart our words, as a hostile
lawyer might in cross-examining a witness. Rather than be
abashed at our ignorance, we should be happy that there is always more to discover in the Bible and we should rejoice when
we do succeed in plumbing a little deeper into its meaning.

Born of the Virgin Mary

"Behold, you will conceive in your womb and bear a son, and you shall name him Jesus. He will be great and will be called Son of the Most High. . . ." But Mary said to the angel, "How can this be, since I have no relations with a man?" And the angel said to her in reply, "The holy Spirit will come upon you, and the power of the Most High will overshadow you. Therefore the child to be born will be called holy, the Son of God" (Lk 1:31-32,34-35).

In the Nicene Creed we profess that Jesus Christ "was born of the Virgin Mary." What are we professing when we say that Jesus was born of a virgin, beyond simply as affirming this as a historical fact?

As with other truths of our faith, different ages have placed the accent on different facets of meaning. St. Augustine taught that original sin was transmitted from generation to generation through sexual intercourse, and therefore viewed Jesus' virginal conception as guaranteeing his freedom from original sin. St. Jerome wrote, *"Omnis coitus immundus"*: All intercourse is unclean, impure, foul. If sexual relations within marriage are viewed as at best a necessary evil to continue the human race, Mary is to be lauded for having refrained from them.

We certainly laud Mary today, but not because she avoided the "defilement" of a normal marriage relationship. Without in any way denigrating the value of celibacy, we do not look upon sexual intercourse within marriage as intrinsically base or impure. Therefore, when we recite the creed and profess that Jesus "was born of the Virgin Mary," we are not putting the accent on the evils of sex being avoided in the conception of Jesus.

Interpretations of the virginity of Mary that are based on a negative view of sexual relations would have been a bit foreign to the first generation of Christians as well. Sexual relations within marriage were understood to be part of God's normal plan (see Gn 1:28): Children were a blessing from God (see Lk 11:27), and barrenness a great misfortune (see Lk 1:24-25). How, then, would the first readers of the Gospels have understood Matthew's words, "Behold, the virgin shall be with child and bear a son" (Mt 1:23)?

One factor influencing their interpretation of Mary's virginity would have been their understanding of human reproduction. Since they lacked the insights of modern biology, they thought of the origin of human life by analogy with plant life: A father would sow a seed in a mother, as a farmer in a field. Mothers were passive agents, making no contribution of their own in the conception of a child; a mother merely provided the place where the seed sown by the father would be nourished and grow. The father was the source and agent of life. The bearing of sons provided for the continuation of the father's family and lineage; daughters would marry and be absorbed into other families. Generations were traced primarily from father to son, as the genealogies of Jesus indicate (see Mt 1:1-17; Lk 3:23-38).

To say that Jesus was "born of a virgin" meant that he was not begotten by a human father; to say that he was conceived in Mary through the power of the Most High meant that the source and agent of his life was God: God was his Father. Therefore, as Luke emphasizes, "He will be great and will be called Son of the Most High. . . . The child to be born will be called holy, the Son of God" (Lk 1:32, 35). The lineage of Jesus is traced to God himself, although Joseph provided legal paternity in the line of David.

To say that Jesus Christ was born of a virgin said less about Mary than it did about Jesus: It proclaimed his identity as the Son of God. Of course, it also said something about Mary. But we should not so emphasize what it says about Mary that we overlook what it says about Jesus. The Gospels were written to proclaim who Jesus is, and this they do in telling us that he was born of the Virgin Mary by the power of God: Jesus Christ is the Son of God.

Laid in a Manger

She gave birth to her firstborn son. She wrapped him in swaddling clothes and laid him in a manger, because there was no room for them in the inn (Lk 2:7).

Our culture has seized on Christmas as the Christian feast to celebrate with extravagance. Even families with vague religious beliefs will exchange presents, decorate Christmas trees, and set up manger scenes.

The secular prominence given Christmas today contrasts with the economy with which Scripture describes the original event. Paul mentions in passing that "God sent his Son, born of a woman" (Gal 4:4), but tells us nothing more about the birth of Jesus. The other letters of the New Testament make no mention of it at all, nor do the gospels of Mark and John. Only Matthew and Luke tell us about Jesus' birth — and they tell us surprisingly little about the actual event.

Matthew tells of Mary being found with child through the Holy Spirit and of Joseph being told in a dream to take her as his wife (see Mt 1:18-24). Then Christmas day is covered in one verse: "He had no relations with her until she bore a son, and he named him Jesus" (Mt 1:25). Matthew continues with an account of Magi arriving after Jesus was born (see Mt 2:1) — an event that apparently happened some time after, since Herod will eventually order the murder of all boys born near Bethlehem within the past two years (see Mt 2:16).

Our Christmas cribs portray the Magi adoring the infant Jesus in a manger, but we can wonder whether the Holy Family would still be in emergency quarters for an extended time after Jesus' birth. In fact, Matthew describes the Magi entering a house to see Jesus (see Mt 2:11). Matthew has said nothing about the setting of Jesus' birth; for that we are dependent on Luke.

Luke's account is also brief. Joseph and Mary come from Nazareth to Bethlehem because of a census, and while there, the time came for Mary to give birth (see Lk 2:1-6). "She gave birth to her firstborn son. She wrapped him in swaddling clothes and laid him in a manger, because there was no room for them in the inn" (Lk 2:7). Luke goes on to describe the shepherds seeing angels and finding Jesus "lying in the manger" (Lk 2:12, 16); unlike the Magi, the shepherds arrive quickly at the scene.

But what scene should we visualize them arriving at? Our Christmas sets usually portray it as an animal shelter, usually a thatched hut. An animal shelter is one meaning of the Greek word that Luke uses for manger — but another meaning is a feeding trough for animals. Luke does not say that Jesus was *born* in a manger, but that he was *laid* in a manger after his birth, and found *lying* in a manger by the shepherds. When Luke uses the word *manger*, he has in mind an animal feeding-trough used as a makeshift cradle.

Of course, an animal feeding-trough might naturally be found in an animal shelter. But what kind of shelter should we imagine? The most ancient traditions place the birth of Jesus in a cave, not a hut. This is the testimony of Justin Martyr in the second century and of Origen in the third century; both lived in the Holy Land and would have known local traditions. Indeed, the Church of the Nativity in Bethlehem is built over a cave as the birthplace of Jesus.

Caves were commonly used not only as animal shelters but also as living quarters by ordinary people at the time of Jesus. Hence the ancient traditions are consistent with Luke's account: Joseph may have taken Mary to a cave, otherwise used as an animal shelter, for her to give birth to Jesus; there she laid him in a manger.

He through whom the world was created was cradled in an animal feeding-trough — a mystery and marvel to ponder!

You Are Salt

"You are the salt of the earth. But if salt loses its taste, with what can it be seasoned? It is no longer good for anything but to be thrown out and trampled underfoot" (Mt 5:13 NIV).

These familiar words of Jesus are puzzling if we try to understand them too literally. What does it mean to be "the salt of the earth"?

If we mix salt in our gardens our plants will soon die. We are told that after Rome captured and destroyed Carthage they plowed salt into its fields to prevent crops from ever being raised there again. This does not seem to be what Jesus had in mind in calling his disciples "the salt of the earth."

His words about salt becoming tasteless (or "losing its savor" in older translations) are equally puzzling. Salt is a simple chemical compound and cannot lose its characteristic taste without ceasing to be salt. We could more easily speak about water losing its wetness or flames losing their heat.

But if these phrases are puzzling if understood too literally, they are rich in symbolic meaning. If we are salt, then what is our savor? What is it that is most characteristic of us as followers of Christ?

We might first think of our faith, our living relationship with Christ. For us to let our faith wither and our relationship with Christ grow cold would be like salt losing its taste: It would no longer be salt, and we would no longer be Christians. What would it profit us to gain the whole world but lose our personal relationship with Christ?

Our saltiness is also our zeal in serving Christ. This should be so intrinsic to our relationship with Christ and flow so naturally from it that for us to lose our zeal as his followers would be like salt losing its taste or water losing its wetness. If we are no longer moved to serve him who has given us life, then we have become literally "good for nothing" in his kingdom. A lukewarm or indifferent disciple is as much a contradiction as is tasteless salt.

What then does it mean to be "the salt of the earth"? Here also some symbolic meanings suggest themselves, even if we are puzzled by the literal meaning.

We naturally think of salt as what flavors and preserves food. Even a little bit of salt can make quite a difference in how food tastes. Try cooking your oatmeal without salt sometime and see!

This naturally suggests comparing salt with yeast: A little bit of each makes a great deal of difference in how our cooking turns out. Jesus spoke of the kingdom of heaven as a small amount of yeast that leavens a whole batch of dough (see Mt 13:33). So too with us as salt: We are meant to (figuratively) be the salt of the earth in a manner like the action of yeast as leaven. We are meant to be a transforming presence in the world, helping to bring the kingdom of heaven to earth. We are meant to make a difference in the lives of those around us.

Mark's Gospel preserves an enigmatic saying of Jesus: "Everyone will be salted with fire" (Mk 9:49 NIV). This verse has been understood (or not understood) in quite different ways; we may be justified in at least seeing a link between salt and fire in it.

John the Baptist foretold that Jesus would baptize with "the Holy Spirit and with fire" (Mt 3:11 NIV). Fire is the fire of judgment, but it is also a symbol of the divine life within us. It is the presence of the Holy Spirit within us that unites us with Christ and makes us children of God — the Holy Spirit that fell as tongues of fire on Pentecost. So to be "salted with fire" suggests receiving a spark of divine life. If we lose this savor of divine life, then we are as tasteless salt.

Fire is also contagious. A tiny spark can start a huge blaze

— just as the bit of yeast can leaven the whole batch of bread. The spark of divine life within us is meant to be contagious and to enflame those around us; the fire of the Spirit within us is meant to enkindle the earth.

Jesus said, "I have come to bring fire on the earth, and how I wish it were already kindled!" (Lk 12:49 NIV). But this fire upon the earth will not fall from heaven as a blazing comet crashing into our planet; rather God's plan that it be the result of the spark of divine life within each of us, joining with others to transform the world with the love of God.

We are the salt of the earth: We have the fire of divine life that Jesus longs to see engulf the earth.

The Pharisees

"Two people went up to the temple area to pray; one was a Pharisee and the other was a tax collector. The Pharisee took up his position and spoke this prayer to himself, 'O God, I thank you that I am not like the rest of humanity — greedy, dishonest, adulterous — or even like this tax collector. I fast twice a week, and I pay tithes on my whole income.' But the tax collector stood off at a distance and would not even raise his eyes to heaven but beat his breast and prayed, 'O God, be merciful to me a sinner.' I tell you, the latter went home justified, not the former; for everyone who exalts himself will be humbled, and the one who humbles himself will be exalted" (Lk 18:10-14).

When we hear the word *Pharisee* what comes to our minds? Probably ideas like "hypocrisy," "self-righteousness," and "enemies of Jesus." But those impressions do not give us a very accurate view of the Pharisees. If we think of the Pharisees only in negative terms, then the parable of the two men praying in the temple loses much of the impact it should have for us.

Who were the Pharisees? Their origin seems to lie in a popular movement of piety among Jews about two hundred years before the time of Jesus. The books of Maccabees mention Jewish *Hasideans* who fought against Syrian rulers when they tried to outlaw Jewish observances. The name *Hasidean* comes from the Hebrew word for *pious*. The Pharisees are thought to have evolved from this group of pious Jews who opposed pagan influences.

The Pharisees were what we would call today a "grassroots movement." They were not a part of the religious or political establishment of Judaism. They were a "lay movement" within Judaism, since they were led not by priests but by lay teachers. Their overriding concern was to obey all that God asked of them, and they found his will indicated both in the written law (the books of Moses) and in the oral traditions that had grown up around the law. They traced these oral traditions back to Moses himself. The Pharisees were very concerned to live holy lives in accordance with God's laws and to hold themselves aloof from all uncleanness.

Not every Jew saw things that same way, or was zealous about living a blameless life. Some Jews accepted only the written law as fully binding, and rejected part or all of the oral law. Other Jews were simply lax about obeying the law in any form. The Pharisees seemed to have pulled away from those who were lukewarm or who disagreed with their understanding of oral tradition; the word *Pharisee* itself seems to come from the Aramaic word for *separated ones*.

Tragically, the Pharisees' attempt at righteousness sometimes became self-righteousness, and some Pharisees scorned those who did not live up to their standard. Luke introduces Jesus' parable of the two men praying in the temple with the words "He then addressed this parable to those who were convinced of their own righteousness and despised everyone else" (Lk 18:9).

The main point Jesus makes in telling the parable is that we achieve righteousness before God not from our own activity but by a contrite recognition of our sinfulness and by asking for his mercy. Secondly, the parable condemns the Pharisee's sense of superiority over the tax collector, adding a warning that is also sounded elsewhere in the Gospels: "Everyone who exalts himself will be humbled, and the one who humbles himself will be exalted" (Lk 18:14).

This parable can take on pointed meaning for us if we examine our own similarities with the Pharisees. Were the Pharisees eager to do God's will as they understood it? So presumably are we. Were the Pharisees convinced that they understood God's way for them, and that those who saw things differently were wrong? We may have a corresponding self-assurance. Did the Pharisees lament the lukewarmness of their fellow Jews and hold themselves aloof from them? We may be tempted to similar attitudes about fellow Christians. And from there it is but a very short step to thinking ourselves as pleasing to God and others as less pleasing — which was the attitude of the Pharisee in Jesus' parable.

If we think Jesus' parable about this Pharisee doesn't really apply to us, perhaps that is a sign it does.

Render to God

Then the Pharisees went out and laid plans to trap him in his words. They sent their disciples to him along with the Herodians. "Teacher," they said, "we know you are a man of integrity and that you teach the way of God in accordance with the truth. You aren't swayed by men, because you pay no attention to who they are. Tell us then, what is your opinion? Is it right to pay taxes to Caesar or not?" But Jesus, knowing their evil intent, said, "You hypocrites, why are you trying to trap me? Show me the coin used for paying the tax." They brought him a denarius, and he asked them, "Whose portrait is this? And whose inscription?" "Caesar's," they replied. Then he said to them, "Give to Caesar what is Caesar's, and to God what is God's" (Mt 22:15-22 NIV).

As Jesus immediately recognized, the question put to him was addressed in bad faith and was designed to trip him up. Taxes are never popular, but the Roman tax that the questioners had in mind was especially unpopular. It had been imposed in connection with the census of Quirinius mentioned in Luke 2:1-5, and had given rise to a revolt led by Judas the Galilean. This Judas taught that Jews should not pay taxes to Caesar and started a rebellion against the Romans; his rebellion is referred to in Acts 5:37.

If Jesus came out against paying taxes to the Roman emperor, his enemies could accuse him of treason — of being just one more rabble-rouser from Galilee (see Lk 20:20; 23:2). But if Jesus upheld the payment of taxes to Rome, he would be upholding the rule of a pagan emperor over a kingdom promised to King David and his successors, and he would discredit himself in the eyes of all who were looking to him for political liberation.

Jesus skillfully escaped the trap that had been set for him. But what is the meaning of his answer for us? How do we determine what belongs to Caesar and what belongs to God?

We should first note that Jesus was not talking about what we think of as the separation of church and state. This is a modern Western notion which would have been quite foreign to the way people thought at the time of Jesus. Indeed, it is still a foreign way of thinking in many countries today — in Islamic countries, for example. At the time of Jesus it was simply assumed that what we think of as religion and what we think of as politics would be closely intertwined, and Jesus did not intend his reply to challenge this assumption.

The key to understanding Jesus' reply lies in his requests: "Show me the coin used for paying the tax . . . Whose portrait is this? And whose inscription?" The coin used for paying the Roman tax was the silver denarius, minted in Rome but in common use in Judea at the time of Jesus. It carried the image of the Roman emperor, along with the inscription, "Tiberius Caesar, son of the deified Augustus."

Such an image and inscription were like a property seal on a bit of precious metal. We might think of a property seal as being similar to the imprint of a signet ring on a blob of wax sealing a letter. It was a personal mark which indicated the owner of whatever object bore it. And in the case of the discs of precious metal which were used as coins, the image and inscription of Caesar meant that the coins belonged to Caesar: He had minted them.

Jesus' reply to the question put to him meant therefore: Give back to Caesar what already belongs to him, but don't forget to give to God what belongs to God.

And what does belong to God? What bears the image of God and carries his property seal?

We do! "So God created man in his own image, in the image of God he created him; male and female he created them" (Gn 1:27 NIV). We have been minted by God, minted in his image. We therefore fundamentally belong to God, and God has a legitimate right to have his lordship over us recognized. Just as we must render to each person his due and give him what belongs to him (including Caesar), so we must render to God what belongs to him — and this is ourselves above all else, for we have been created by him and bear his image.

Jesus therefore did more than escape a trap. He raised a question about taxation to the highest question that faces us: the question of our acknowledging God's claim over us.

Talents and Charisms

"It will be as when a man who was going on a journey called in his servants and entrusted his possessions to them. To one he gave five talents; to another, two; to a third, one — to each according to his ability. Then he went away. Immediately the one who received five talents went and traded with them, and made another five" (Mt 25:14-16).

The meaning of words can change with time. For us a *talent* is a natural ability or special aptitude: "She has a real talent for playing the piano." But in very ancient times a talent was a unit of weight, equal to the load a person could carry, or roughly sixty-five pounds. By New Testament times, the word had come to connote this weight of gold or silver, and therefore was a measure of wealth. It has this meaning in the parable of the talents: Three men are given various sizable sums of money to invest during their master's absence.

Writers in the Middle Ages, with Jesus' parable of the talents in mind, began to use the word *talent* as a poetic expression for endowments and abilities that one had been given. Their figurative use eventually became the common meaning of the word. The origins of this meaning in Jesus' parable still linger, for our notion of talent is related to the idea of gift: To say "She is a gifted pianist" means much the same as to say "She is a talented pianist."

The word *charism* has also undergone some evolution in meaning. It first occurs in the letters of Paul. He may have invented the word, or he may have adopted it from the colloquial Greek of his day. In either case, charism (Greek *charisma*) is related to the Greek word *charis*, which means favor, graciousness, or grace. For Paul, a charism was an effect of God's favor or grace; it was a gift of God to us, or something that God did for us out of love.

The word *charism* had very broad meaning for Paul. He could say that "the gift [*charisma*] of God is eternal life in Christ Jesus" (Rom 6:23), and he could speak of his getting out of jail as a "gift [*charisma*] granted us through the prayers of many" (2 Cor 1:11). Paul also described the various ways that the Holy Spirit worked through Christians as charisms (see 1 Cor 12:4-31). But Paul did not restrict the word *charism* to the charisms of 1 Corinthians 12. For Paul, eternal life and escape from jail were also examples of charisms — gifts from God.

If we look at their origins, talent and charism are different words for much the same reality. The essential note is that of "givenness": Talents/charisms are given us by God. Furthermore, they have been given to us so that we can make good use of them. That is the point of Jesus' parable of the talents, and that is likewise a point Paul makes: " Since we have gifts that differ according to the grace given to us, let us exercise them" (Rom 12:6).

Today, however, we think of talents and charisms as two different realities. For us a talent is a natural ability, like being a good speaker, and a charism is a supernatural ability, like the gift of healing. While a distinction can be drawn between the natural and the supernatural, it is not a distinction that Jesus or Paul wanted to make when they spoke of talents and charisms. Nor is it always an easy line to draw in practice. Where does one's talent for teaching leave off and one's charism of teaching (see Rom 12:7) begin?

It is probably more fruitful to think of both talents and charisms as abilities we have been given by God, to be used in his service and for the good of others. We can understand Jesus' parable of the talents as an exhortation to make use of our gifts, our charisms. And we can take Paul's instructions about the use of charisms as encompassing even what we might think of as our natural talents. They, too, have been given us by God, and are meant to be used in service.

He Is Our Peace

"The Advocate, the holy Spirit that the Father will send in my name — he will teach you everything and remind you of all that [I] told you. Peace I leave with you; my peace I give to you. Not as the world gives do I give it to you" (Jn 14:26-27).

During the Last Supper, Jesus told his followers that he would shortly leave them, and spoke of farewell gifts that he would leave in his place. He promised his followers that he would send them the Holy Spirit, and that he would give them a peace that was unlike the peace of this world.

We may have thought about the gift of the Holy Spirit — but what about Christ's gift of peace? What is the peace that is unlike the peace of the world? And how are the gift of the Spirit and the gift of peace related?

A good starting point for understanding Jesus' promise of peace is the word itself. Jesus spoke Aramaic, a language related to Hebrew. In Aramaic and Hebrew, the word for peace is much the same; we have probably heard it in its Hebrew form — *shalom*. The root meaning of *shalom* is the notion of being complete or whole; the Hebrew idea of peace is not simply the absence of strife, but a state of fulfillment.

To give a down-to-earth example: I have a thick Hebrew-English dictionary whose Hebrew title is *A Shalem Hebrew-English Dictionary*, with *shalem* being the adjective form of the noun *shalom*. The title does not mean that this dictionary is free of conflict, but that it is a complete dictionary — we would say unabridged. Other Hebrew words built on the same root as *shalom* carry connotations of wholeness, soundness, perfection.

The peace that Christ gives us is therefore not primarily a

matter of absence of strife, but a state of completeness, wholeness, fulfillment. In such a state there is no conflict, but peace in its biblical sense is more basically a matter of fulfillment.

What is this state of fulfillment that Christ left with his followers as his gift to them? An answer lies in Paul's letter to the Ephesians, chapter 2, verses 14 to 18: "For he is our peace, he who made both one and broke down the dividing wall of enmity, through his flesh, abolishing the law with its commandments and legal claims, that he might create in himself one new person in place of the two, thus establishing peace, and might reconcile both with God, in one body, through the cross, putting that enmity to death by it. He came and preached peace to you who were far off and peace to those who were near, for through him we both have access in one Spirit to the Father."

Paul is speaking of the reconciliation in Christ of Gentiles with Jews. This results in peace in the sense of absence of conflict, but this peace is achieved through our common incorporation into Christ; he is our peace, making us one by incorporating us into one body, his body. And more important than our being reconciled with one another is our being reconciled with God through the cross of Christ. Our reconciliation with God means that we now have access to him — and this access is in the Holy Spirit, given to us by Christ.

In other words, the peace that we have in Christ is the result of his whole redemptive work. It is our being filled with the Holy Spirit and reconciled with God and with one another. The peace of Christ is what results from our being incorporated into his body and reconciled as a body with his Father. The peace of Christ is the fulfillment of his work; it is also our being made whole through receiving the Holy Spirit.

Since the Holy Spirit completes the work of Christ and brings it to fulfillment, it is no accident that Jesus spoke both of his gift of the Spirit and of his gift of peace during the Last Supper. One involves the other. We are incorporated into Christ through the Holy Spirit — and it is precisely this incorporation which Paul speaks of when he says that Christ is our peace.

Arise!

People . . . arrived and said, "Your daughter has died; why trouble the teacher any longer?" Disregarding the message that was reported, Jesus said to the synagogue official, "Do not be afraid; just have faith."
. . . He took the child by the hand and said to her, "Talitha koum," which means, "Little girl, I say to you, arise!" The girl, a child of twelve, arose immediately and walked around (Mk 5:35-36, 41-42).

Easter is the season of celebrating the resurrection of Jesus Christ, and celebrating as well our own hope of rising with him. If Jesus had not risen from the dead, our faith would be in vain and we would have no hope of resurrection (see 1 Cor 15:12-18). But since Christ is risen, we who are joined with him through baptism "shall also be united with him in the resurrection" (Rom 6:5).

Seen in the light of Easter, Jesus' raising of the daughter of Jairus is a prefigurement of our own resurrection. The girl was dead and the neighborhood was mourning her, but Jesus said, "Why this commotion and weeping? The child is not dead but asleep" (Mk 5:39). Jesus was not denying the reality of her death, but saying that her death, like sleep, would come to an end. He would awaken her from death by a word, just as one calls upon the sleeping to arise.

The word Jesus used was *koum,* the ordinary Aramaic word for *get up* or *arise*. Mark translated Jesus' words into Greek for the benefit of readers who did not know Aramaic: He "said to her, '*Talitha koum,*' which means, 'Little girl, I say to you, arise!' "

Mark's translation would have been a signal to his readers that there was a deeper meaning in this event than solely the restoration of life to this girl. The Greek verb that Mark used to translate Jesus' command of "Arise!" is the same Greek verb that is used in the New Testament for Jesus' own resurrection. Jesus was raised from the dead; Jesus raised this girl from the dead — and Jesus will raise us from the dead.

Jairus was not the only official in Capernaum to seek the help of Jesus in the face of death. A Roman centurion stationed in Capernaum had a servant who was "ill and about to die" (Lk 7:2). When Jesus said he would come and cure him, the centurion replied, "Lord, do not trouble yourself, for I am not worthy to have you enter under my roof. Therefore, I did not consider myself worthy to come to you; but say the word and let my servant be healed" (Lk 7:6-7).

Our prayer at Mass before Communion echoes the centurion: "Lord, I am not worthy to receive you, but only say the word and I shall be healed." One day in reciting this prayer, the question occurred to me: Just what is the word that I am imploring Jesus to say in order that I would be healed? The parallel between the two officials from Capernaum came to mind, and I realized that in echoing the centurion's request I was really asking for the word that Jesus spoke to the synagogue official's daughter. The word I need Jesus to say to me is "*Koum*" — "Arise!"

"Only say the word and I shall be healed." Ultimately the healing we need from Jesus is not from arthritis or heart disease, or from this or that sin, but the full healing of resurrection. We need and welcome his partial healings along the way to resurrection, but they are only partial. He may heal us of our ailments, but the way of all flesh nevertheless leads to death. He forgives our sins, but we find ourselves committing them again, or finding new ones to commit. We will always stand in need of physical and spiritual healing until we are granted the ultimate and final healing of resurrection, freeing us forever from sin and pain.

We therefore pray to the risen Jesus: Speak your word *koum* to me; command me to arise. Raise me up now from my sins and illnesses. Raise me up on the last day to eternal life. Say only the word "Arise!", and I shall truly be healed.

8

My Thoughts Are
Not Your Thoughts

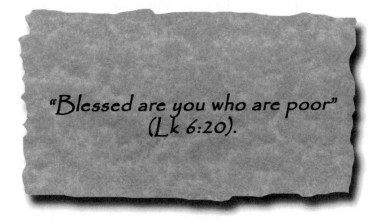

"Blessed are you who are poor"
(Lk 6:20).

Happy Are You

Then fixing his eyes on his disciples he said:
"How happy are you who are poor: yours is the kingdom of God.

"Happy you who are hungry now: you shall be satisfied.

"Happy you who weep now: you shall laugh.

"Happy are you when people hate you, drive you out, abuse you, denounce your name as criminal, on account of the Son of Man. Rejoice when that day comes and dance for joy, for then your reward will be great in heaven. This was the way their ancestors treated the prophets.

"But alas for you who are rich: you are having your consolation now.

"Alas for you who have your fill now: you shall go hungry.

"Alas for you who laugh now: you shall mourn and weep.

"Alas for you when the world speaks well of you! This was the way their ancestors treated the false prophets" (Lk 6:20-26 JB).

The beatitudes are such a familiar part of our religious heritage that we might miss their meaning. When we read them in Scripture or hear them read during the liturgy, we probably do not wince or squirm very much. That could be a sign that we are missing the point.

Consider: Which of us, if asked whether we would rather be hungry and malnourished or go into a restaurant and order whatever we wanted, would spontaneously choose to go hungry? Yet Jesus says that the hungry person is more fortunate, and the well-fed person is in a sorry state.

Consider: Most of us work hard for a living and try to make our money stretch as far as possible. Few of us strive to give away every cent we have; few of us have poverty as our goal in life. Yet Jesus blesses the poor, and says alas to the rich.

Consider: All of us choose happiness over sorrow; few of us think it is better for us to be abused than complimented. But Jesus' values seem to be just the opposite.

Was Jesus simply exaggerating in order to make a point? Did hunger pains hurt any less back then? Did the rich of his time live more comfortable lives than middle-class Americans do today? How are we to take his words seriously, as a word directing us how to live?

When Jesus spoke these words, they did describe fairly well the state of some of his disciples. Those who left what they had to follow him were dependent on the generosity of others. And when these words of Jesus were repeated in the early Church and written down by Luke, Christians were still far more often persecuted than praised. First-century Christians probably didn't have the problems with this teaching of Jesus that we do; for them, the beatitudes were a word of consolation, not condemnation.

For us today, if we take them seriously, they are a far harder word. They must be understood within the context of Jesus' other hard words: the call to lay down our lives, the invitation to take up our cross and follow Jesus, the warning that the disciple is not above the master. And like these other hard teachings of Jesus, their dominant message is one of hope. Those who lay down their lives shall discover true life; those who follow in the footsteps of Jesus to Calvary will experience resurrection; those who imitate Jesus will be united with him. The beatitudes are true blessings; even the four alases in Luke's version serve only as warnings, lest we miss the blessing God intends for us.

The beatitudes should give us pause. They are a call to the mystery of the cross. They challenge our normal values and thinking. They challenge us to reexamine our lives in the light of Christ. They force us to confront whether we are guided by the Gospel or by the pattern set by the society around us.

The beatitudes should stun us and make us turn to the Lord for direction, asking him how we are to live according to his values. If we hear the word of Jesus in the beatitudes correctly, with the full force of their meaning, we can only drop to our knees in humble acknowledgment that we have far to go in letting our lives be remade and reformed according to the Gospel.

John's Question

When John heard in prison what Christ was doing, he sent his disciples to ask him, "Are you the one who was to come, or should we expect someone else?" Jesus replied, "Go back and report to John what you hear and see: The blind receive sight, the lame walk, those who have leprosy are cured, the deaf hear, the dead are raised, and the good news is preached to the poor. Blessed is the man who does not fall away on account of me" (Mt 11:2-6 NIV).

At first reading, both John the Baptist's question and Jesus' reply are puzzling. Why should John ask whether Jesus is the Messiah: Had not John already proclaimed Jesus to be the one who would baptize with the Holy Spirit and fire (see Mt 3:11)? And in responding, why would Jesus list the works he was doing, since John already knew about these works (see Mt 11:2)? And why would Jesus be worried about being the source of scandal?

John had indeed announced the coming of one more powerful than himself, one who would bring the Holy Spirit (see Mt 3:11), and John had recognized Jesus as this person (see Mt 3:14). But it also seems that John expected this person to execute God's judgment upon the world: "The ax is already at the root of the trees, and every tree that does not produce good fruit will be cut down and thrown into the fire. . . . He will baptize you with the Holy Spirit and with fire. His winnowing fork is in his hand, and he will clear his threshing floor, gathering his wheat into the barn and burning up the chaff with unquenchable fire" (Mt 3:10, 11-12 NIV).

Jesus didn't act as John expected him to act as the Messiah. Jesus passed up opportunities to condemn sinners (see Jn 8:10-11) and instead created opportunities to associate with them (see Lk 19:1-10). Jesus' attitude toward sinners scandalized the Pharisees (see Mt 9:10-13) and may have scandalized John the Baptist as well — or at least disappointed him. Rather than wielding an ax or burning chaff in fire, Jesus fulfilled Isaiah's prophecy, "A bruised reed he will not break, and a smoldering wick he will not snuff out" (Is 42:3).

Jesus in his answer to John the Baptist repeats what John already knows, but describes his actions in terms that echo the prophecies of Isaiah (see Is 29:18-19; 35:5-6; 61:1). Jesus thereby does claim to be the Messiah, the one whose coming was prophesied in the Old Testament. But Jesus comes as the servant of God, the one who will bear the sins of others rather than punish them for their sins (see Is 42:1-4; 52:13-53:12). He came not to condemn but to save (see Jn 3:17).

Jesus did not live up to the expectations of others — not the Pharisees, nor his apostles (who expected him to inaugurate an earthly kingdom; see Acts 1:6), nor even John the Baptist. Hence Jesus said, Blessed is he who is not scandalized by what I do, who does not take offense at the kind of Messiah I am. Happy is the one who believes in me for who I am and who my works reveal me to be.

But what then of John's prophecy of what Jesus would do? If Jesus did not go about separating the wheat from the chaff and burning the chaff, was John's prophecy false? No, it was a true prophecy — but John did not understand the time of its fulfillment.

Jesus did speak of judgment, but of judgment at the end of time (see Mt 25:31-46). His parable of the weeds sown in the field (see Mt 13:24-30) ends with these weeds being burned but forbids their being uprooted before the final harvest, lest the wheat also be harmed. The parable of the net thrown into the sea (see Mt 13:47-50) is also a parable of judgment, but likewise judgment "at the end of the age" (Mt

13:49). Not until then would John's prophecy be completely fulfilled. In the meantime, the work of Jesus is to search out and save the lost (see Lk 19:10). Jesus' urging of his followers to be cautious in passing judgment on others (see Mt 7:1-5) should be understood in this light.

If even John the Baptist could apparently be mistaken in his expectations of Jesus, how much more easily can we fail to understand him! The antidote must be to ponder the pages of the Gospels and meditate on how Jesus acted and what he taught.

That was Jesus' reply to John: Look at what I do, and listen to what I say. Don't make me conform to what you think I must or should be like, but see what I am like. Blessed are you if you can believe in me as I really am. Happy are you who are not scandalized by the way I act but see my actions as a revelation of my loving Father. Happy are you who find eternal life in me.

Wages

"For the kingdom of heaven is like a landowner who went out early in the morning to hire men to work in his vineyard. He agreed to pay them a denarius for the day and sent them into his vineyard. . . . About the eleventh hour he went out and found still others standing around. He said to them, 'You also go and work in my vineyard.' When evening came, the owner of the vineyard said to his foreman, 'Call the workers and pay them their wages.' The workers who were hired about the eleventh hour came and each received a denarius. So when those came who were hired first, they expected to receive more. But each of them also received a denarius. When they received it, they began to grumble against the landowner. 'These men who were hired last worked only one hour,' they said, 'and you have made them equal to us who have borne the burden of the work and the heat of the day.' But he answered one of them, 'Friend, I am not being unfair to you. Didn't you agree to work for a denarius? . . . I want to give the man who was hired last the same as I have you. Don't I have the right to do what I want with my own money? Or are you envious because I am generous?' " (Mt 20:1-15 NIV, shortened).

Jesus' parable of the workers in the vineyard usually troubles us. We instinctively want to side with those who worked hard all day, only to be paid no more than those who slept late, enjoyed a leisurely lunch, and only showed up at work an hour before quitting time.

No matter what explanation is offered, something in us wants to say, "But it's *still* not fair!" Even if the owner is free to do what he wants with his money, and even if those hired first were paid all they agreed to work for, decency (if not justice) demands that those who worked hard be paid more than those who did barely anything.

The rightness or wrongness of this vineyard owner's action is somewhat secondary, however: Jesus' parable is not about human justice but divine mercy. It is the kingdom of heaven that Jesus is teaching about, not labor/management relations.

The denarius — a standard day's wage — can be understood as entrance into this kingdom; the day which we have to work is our lifetime. To receive a day's wage thus means receiving eternal life by participating in the resurrection of Jesus to everlasting glory. Perhaps there are degrees of glory — but the essential thing is to rise with Jesus. The real contrast is between life and death, between being paid eternal wages and not being paid anything at all. In that light the exact amount one is paid is secondary.

We have our whole lifetime to "work out [our] salvation with fear and trembling" (Phil 2:12 NIV). But some of us squander our work time with long coffee breaks and other interruptions. Others do not hear or heed the invitation to the vineyard of the Lord until late in their lives. So, yes, some do bear the heat of the day more than others; some seem to make greater sacrifices for the sake of the kingdom.

The basic point of Jesus' parable, however, is that God is eager to give everyone the basic wage of eternal life in his kingdom. He is not looking for an excuse to pay less than this minimum wage; the vineyard owner certainly would have had a legitimate excuse to pay less to those who worked less. God rather seems to be looking for an excuse to give full wages to as many as possible.

This is borne out by the eleventh-hour wages paid to a criminal who was crucified next to Jesus. This criminal had led a life of violence, and by his own admission he deserved severe punishment. But in what was certainly a last-moment conversion, he turned to Jesus and made the simple plea, "Remember me when you come into your kingdom" (Lk 23:42 NIV). Jesus replied by assuring him that he would enter the kingdom: He would receive the wage of eternal life.

God's eagerness to give us the wage of eternal life does not mean that we should take it for granted or take this life easy. For, in truth, the wage God wants to pay us is far beyond anything we could ever earn. Our work and our efforts are simply our feeble response to his goodness. We should work hard because we know that, no matter how long or diligently we work, we can never earn the wage he gives us.

Nor should we be jealous of those who receive this eternal wage at the eleventh hour. We should rather rejoice with them that they are rescued from death and given life. Did Mary at the foot of the cross feel jealous of the thief whom Jesus pardoned? Neither should we be jealous that God is generous in mercy and forgiveness; rather we should rejoice in his generosity.

Wealth

"The ground of a certain rich man produced a good crop. He thought to himself, 'What shall I do? I have no place to store my crops.'

"Then he said, 'This is what I'll do. I will tear down my barns and build bigger ones, and there I will store all my grain and my goods. And I'll say to myself, "You have plenty of good things laid up for many years. Take life easy; eat, drink and be merry."'

"But God said to him, 'You fool! This very night your life will be demanded from you. Then who will get what you have prepared for yourself?'

"This is how it will be with anyone who stores up things for himself but is not rich toward God" (Lk 12:16-21 NIV).

This parable can be a hard saying for anyone struggling to make a living today, trying to keep pace with bills, working to save enough to be able to afford a down payment for a house. On the one hand, it takes all our effort just to make our income stretch to cover our obligations. On the other hand, Jesus seems to condemn a man who did prudent financial planning.

What was the man in the parable to do? His barns weren't big enough to hold his harvest, so he built bigger barns. Would we have done differently? Would we condemn any farmer who did the same today? It would be irresponsible for a farmer not to make provision for storing his harvest; it would be irresponsible to leave it exposed to the weather and to rot.

The fault of the rich man in the parable does not lie in what he did, but in what he did not do, and in his attitudes. He considered his wealth to be his own, to do with what he liked. He thought that his wealth would assure a safe and comfortable life. He intended to use his wealth solely for his own pleasure.

Jesus points out the illusion of believing that wealth can provide security and happiness. No matter how thick the bank vault and how much money we have in it, wealth cannot make us secure; our lives are in the hands of God. For someone who wants to be completely independent, this must be a disappointment. But for someone who is willing to trust God, this can be a great relief. Our Father in heaven knows our needs; there is no need for us to be anxious.

Jesus says that it is the pagans of this world who set their hearts on what they will eat and drink (see Lk 12:30). This does not mean that Christians will end up having less to eat than pagans, or that Christians will not have to work at jobs like pagans have to, or that Christians should have smaller barns than pagans. It means that Christians should never look to money (or to large, well-filled barns) for the security that only our Father can give.

The rich man of the parable did not intend to use his wealth to benefit anyone but himself. Jesus did not address in this parable our obligation to share our resources with those in need, but he did elsewhere in his teaching. Another rich man was told to give it to the poor (see Lk 18:22-23); the Good Samaritan was held up as an example of helping someone in need even at the price of self-sacrifice (see Lk 10:30-37); Jesus taught that it is through giving alms that we lay up a treasure that is safe from theft and corruption (see Lk 12:33).

In contrast, the rich man of this parable only thinks of himself and his own pleasure. Perhaps he would have been commended by Jesus if he had said to himself, "This is what I will do: I will modestly enlarge my barns to help hold this bountiful harvest, but I will give away to the poor that which is beyond my needs. I will say to myself, Rejoice in God who has been so generous in his blessing. And now that I do not need to work so hard, I will spend more time with my wife and children."

Our first step in learning what is God's will for our wealth is to acknowledge that this is indeed something that we need to find out. If we want Jesus Christ to be the Lord of our life, we cannot separate our possessions and our financial goals from his lordship.

Listen to Him

After six days Jesus took Peter, James and John with him and led them up a high mountain, where they were all alone. There he was transfigured before them. His clothes became dazzling white, whiter than anyone in the world could bleach them. . . . Then a cloud appeared and enveloped them, and a voice came from the cloud: "This is my Son, whom I love. Listen to him!" (Mk 9:2-3, 7 NIV).

If we compare the accounts in Mark's Gospel of Jesus' baptism and of his transfiguration, similarities and differences emerge.

The Father speaks from heaven on both occasions — the only times that we hear the Father speaking in Mark's Gospel. On both occasions the Father states that Jesus is his Son, his beloved (see Mk 1:11; 9:7).

But whereas the Father speaks to Jesus at the time of his baptism ("You are my Son"), during the transfiguration he speaks to Peter and James and John: "This is my Son, whom I love." And at the transfiguration the Father adds an admonition, again clearly addressed to the three apostles: "Listen to him!"

This command to listen to Jesus was not merely a command for Peter, James, and John, but a command for all who would follow Jesus. Its importance was underlined by the fact that it was the Father himself giving this command, and giving it in the context of the transfiguration. It is therefore a command that each of us must heed, and heed carefully.

Can we discover more about this command, however? We

know we should listen to whatever Jesus speaks to us through Scripture and the church. But did the Father have something more specific in mind on that occasion? Was he saying to Peter and James and John, "Listen to everything that Jesus teaches," or was he saying more specifically, "Pay particular attention to what Jesus has just taught you and will teach you after you go down from the mountain?"

If we examine Mark's Gospel carefully, we can reasonably interpret the Father's intention to be the latter: "Listen to what Jesus is specifically trying to teach you right now." For the transfiguration occurs right after Jesus' first foretelling of his coming passion and death and shortly before his second warning of how he will die. In each case the disciples fail to understand what Jesus is talking about. They cannot conceive that the Messiah would bring salvation through suffering and death; rather they are hoping to reap personal rewards by following a triumphant Messiah.

Consider the flow of words and events in Mark: Peter acknowledges Jesus as the Messiah (see Mk 8:29); Jesus immediately tells of his coming rejection, suffering, death, and resurrection (see 8:31); Peter refuses to accept this (see 8:32); Jesus rebukes Peter for rejecting God's way (see 8:33); Jesus teaches that anyone who wants to follow him must lay down his life and accept the same fate as he himself will suffer (see 8:34-36).

Jesus is then transfigured (see 9:2-8) and refers once more to his suffering (see 9:12). After expelling a demon that the apostles could not (see 9:14-29), Jesus again speaks of his death (see 9:30-31), but his followers do not understand what he is talking about (see 9:32). They rather get into an argument among themselves over who is greatest (see 9:33-34), an argument Jesus resolves by teaching that anyone who wants to be great must be last and servant of all (see 9:35) — which is to say, must imitate his own example of self-sacrificing service.

It is in the midst of this that the Father says, "Listen to him." From the context we can understand the Father to be saying, "Listen to my Son when he speaks of his mission to serve and when he calls you to serve. Listen to him when he speaks of laying down his own life and when he invites you to lay down your lives in imitation of him.

"Listen to him when he teaches that the path of earthly power and honor is not the path that he will follow as the Messiah and not the path that his followers are to take either. Listen to him when he speaks of his cross and invites you to take up your crosses and follow in his footsteps. Listen to him when he reveals the great mystery that those who lose their lives for his sake will save them.

"Do not be slow to understand; do not be concerned about who is greatest; do not reject the cross. Rather, listen to my beloved Son, and follow the path he is laying out before you."

The Shepherd

"What man among you with a hundred sheep, losing one, would not leave the ninety-nine in the wilderness and go after the missing one till he found it? And when he found it, would he not joyfully take it on his shoulders and then, when he got home, call together his friends and neighbours? 'Rejoice with me,' he would say, 'I have found my sheep that was lost.' In the same way, I tell you, there will be more rejoicing in heaven over one repentant sinner than over ninety-nine virtuous men who have no need of repentance" (Lk 15:4-7 JB).

Jesus invites us to put ourselves in the sandals of this shepherd: "What man among you with a hundred sheep. . . ." So let us imagine that we own a hundred sheep and that one of them is missing. Matthew's Gospel notes that it is not merely lost but "strays" (Mt 18:12 JB).

What would we do if our sheep count came up one short? Some of us might mutter a few curses: We already have more than enough work to do without running around looking for a sheep that didn't have enough sense to stay with the rest of the flock.

Then what? Would we "leave the ninety-nine in the wilderness and go after the missing one"? Probably not. The "wilderness" of Jesus' parable was the rocky hills and ravines of eastern Judea. To leave ninety-nine sheep unguarded in this area is to invite their wandering off in ninety-nine different directions and to place them at the mercy of wolves and robbers. Probably we would say to ourselves, "Well, I am out one sheep, but I still have ninety-nine left, and I have to take care of them." End of story.

But the shepherd in Jesus' parable does not react as we would. He risks the ninety-nine for the sake of the one. He abandons all he has for what he doesn't have.

Let us accompany him on his search, even though we think he is foolish to leave behind the ninety-nine. He eventually finds his lost sheep. What would we do at this point? Probably start kicking the errant sheep in the direction of home, all the while lecturing it about not wandering off again: "You stupid sheep, you made me waste my whole day looking for you." But the shepherd of Jesus' parable "sets it on his shoulders with great joy." Amazing!

And when we arrived home with our lost sheep, what would we tell our neighbors? Wouldn't we complain about all the trouble it caused us, and about how our legs ache from climbing up and down ravines all day? But not this shepherd: He tells his neighbors, "Rejoice with me because I have found my lost sheep."

I therefore believe that Jesus' "What man among you. . . ." is said tongue-in-cheek. Few if any of his listeners, and few if any of us, would have reacted as did this shepherd.

And that is precisely the point that Jesus wishes to make! The shepherd is a biblical symbol of God: "The LORD is my shepherd" (Ps 23:1). God does not treat us as human logic and values might suggest. His thinking is as different from ours as ours is from the shepherd of Jesus' parable.

God is willing to give up what he has — his Son — in order to obtain what he does not have — us. He does not curse us because we have strayed away in sin. Rather he delights in searching us out and rescuing us. He finds joy in finding us. He is so happy to rescue us, even when we are lost through our own fault, that he throws a party in heaven.

Jesus told this parable because he was being criticized for welcoming sinners to himself and eating with them (see Lk

15:2). The parable points out that God is different from what his critics imagined, and if they understood the true nature of God, they would understand why Jesus behaved as he did. God had sent his Son "to seek out and to save what was lost" (Lk 19:10 JB).

If we imagine God in our own image, we might be afraid of his finding us. But if we accept what Jesus tells us about his Father, we will be eager to let him find us, no matter how far we may have strayed.

Eternal Life

"For this is the will of my Father, that everyone who sees the Son and believes in him may have eternal life, and I shall raise him [on] the last day" (Jn 6:40).

Jesus' promise of eternal life transforms the meaning of human life. It challenges every natural assumption and value we might hold. It requires us to radically change our perspective on what is important and what is unimportant.

According to a natural view, life ends with death. Death comes as a tragic separation between lover and beloved, between child and parent, between lifelong friends. Death disrupts the highest human happiness we can experience, the love of two persons for each other.

Sometimes death comes out of season, taking away a young person barely setting out on life. Sometimes death takes away someone we were counting on to help us: a political leader able to arouse hope, a scientist working on a cure for cancer, a writer able to inspire us. And sometimes death comes sadly late and out of season, after an elderly person has declined far from being the person they once were.

If our present life is but a prelude, however, our perspective is radically changed. Then there is no permanent separation between those united in love in Christ. Then we need not lose hope for those whose last years are years of decline: They shall once again be the persons they were, and more. They shall experience a resurrection of their body that frees them from the accumulated disabilities of decades; they shall once again rejoice in the fullness of life.

The perspective of eternity also transforms our view of all

who live in our midst who seem to be short-changed by life. Those born mentally retarded seem condemned to be incomplete persons, unless we can anticipate their completion in eternity. Those who are victims of incurable diseases and birth defects, consigned to a life of dependence, can seem to us cruelly robbed of life, unless we know in faith that such greater fulfillment awaits them that their suffering will be made up for uncountable times.

The perspective of eternity must also shape our view of the unborn. If no spark of human life will ever die out, then the unborn must be reverenced for their life as well as the born. If God can raise up with new bodies for those whose earthly bodies are deformed and ravaged, then he can certainly also give resurrected bodies even to those whose earthly bodies never had a chance to develop fully.

The prospect of eternal life should also change our view of those whose earthly life is one of poverty and suffering. We can have hope that those whose present life is one of misery will find rest and reward in the next life. But even more, the prospect of our sharing eternal life with them should heighten our sense of obligation to them here and now. I cannot turn my back on the suffering and needs of others; I shall be with them in eternity, and must be concerned for them now.

There will be a judgment for each of us as we enter eternal life. We live in hope of passing that judgment, through the redemption that Jesus Christ has given us. We must also hold that hope for others, that they too will be saved through the mystery of God's love for them. Then our expectation can be that those we love now, we will be able to love for all eternity. Our hope can be that those who do not experience the fullness of life on this earth will experience it in the presence of their Father in heaven. We should reverence everyone as intended for resurrection into eternal life with us, in Christ Jesus our Lord.